BETWEEN A
ROCK
— AND A —
HARD
PLACE

BETWEEN A
ROCK
— AND A —
HARD
PLACE

TONY EVANS

MOODY PUBLISHERS

CHICAGO

All Scripture quotations, unless otherwise indicated, are taken from the *New American Standard Bible*®, Copyright ©1960, 1962, 1963, 1968, 1971, 1972, 1973, 1975, 1977, 1995 by The Lockman Foundation. Used by permission. (www.Lockman.org)

Scripture quotations marked KJV are taken from the King James Version.

Edited by Jim Vincent
Interior design: Smartt Guys design
Cover design: Tan Nguyen
Cover image: iStockPhoto

Library of Congress Cataloging-in-Publication Data

Evans, Tony, 1949-
  Between a rock and a hard place / Tony Evans.
    p. cm.
  ISBN 978-0-8024-2326-9
  1. Trust in God—Christianity. 2. Providence and government of God—Christianity. 3. Obedience—Religious aspects—Christianity. 4.Bible—Criticism, interpretation, etc. I. Title.
  BT135.E93 2010
  231'.5—dc22
                                                                              2010017446

We hope you enjoy this book from Moody Publishers. Our goal is to provide high-quality, thought-provoking books and products that connect truth to your real needs and challenges. For more information on other books and products written and produced from a biblical perspective, go to www.moodypublishers.com or write to:

Moody Publishers
820 N. LaSalle Boulevard
Chicago, IL 60610

1 3 5 7 9 10 8 6 4 2

Printed in the United States of America

To my good friend
Coach Bruce Chambers,
who continues to persevere as he lives life
between a rock and a hard place

CONTENTS

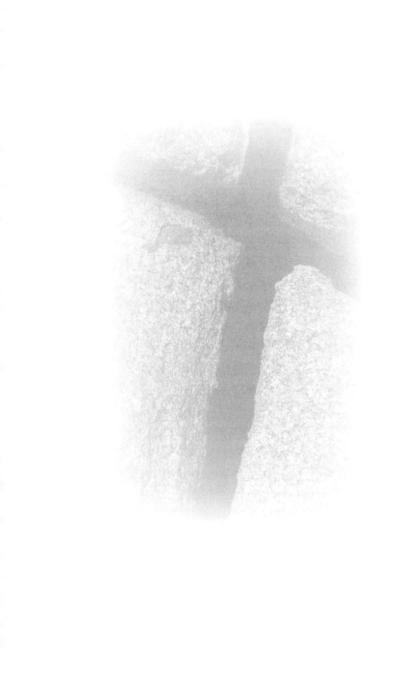

INTRODUCTION

EVERY SUMMER I GO to the doctor's office for an annual medical exam. Of all of the things that my doctor does during that health examination, the one that I despise the most is the stress test. He attaches electronic probes all over my body. Then he sticks me on a treadmill. Next, he makes the treadmill go faster and faster up an incline because he wants to know the real condition of my heart.

My heart might feel fine to me but it might not be fine. The doctor can determine the strength of my heart only when he measures it under stress. So what he does is create a stressful situation: I'm walking for a long period of time, huffing and puffing, climbing a hill that never seems to end. He's testing my heart to see whether how I feel is how I really am. Because it's possible to have good feelings yet still have a bad heart.

Living the Christian life is no different. It's possible to come to church every week, sing worship songs, memorize Bible verses, serve on a variety of committees, and assume that your heart, faith, and soul are strong. It's even easy to say things like, "I love you, God. God, you are so good. I'll follow you, God. I'll do whatever you say."

But God doesn't want to just take your word for it.

He tests you and me because He wants what is best for us. He tests us because He is getting ready to do something amazing in our lives. The way that He tests us is by putting us in a stressful scenario. God puts us on a treadmill. He designs a unique treadmill test to measure and reveal the real condition of our souls.

Much like the stress test my doctor puts me through every summer, God allows trials and tests in our lives in order to reveal where we are along our spiritual journey. He does this for the purpose of correcting whatever happens to be wrong, revealing whatever needs to be exposed, and strengthening whatever seems to be weak so that we might move on to what He has in store for us.

In this book we're going to go deeper into the lives of Bible characters, from Abraham to Mary and Martha, who ended up between a rock and a hard place—pinned in really tough situations. There are a myriad of these types of situations in the Bible. In fact, when I first started studying the Bible early on, I would come across these trials all the time. It didn't take me long to begin to see a pattern emerging as the same type of trial would appear again and again, just with different names and faces.

These were trials where it was not just a person having a problem to deal with, but God was actually creating a scenario where the person was caught between a rock and a hard place. I began to study these scenes very closely, and I discovered patterns that kept coming up in them time and again. God gave such trials to examine and strengthen the faith of those who followed Him.

When we find no clear direction to turn without there being a problem, and when any decision we could make is potentially the wrong one, God is getting ready to do a substantial thing in our lives. Keep this in mind as we go through these different biblical examples of others who were caught between a rock and a hard place. Keep this in mind because, with this guiding principle of truth, we can find hope and peace in the middle of a trial. God *will* use that hard place to do something significant in our lives.

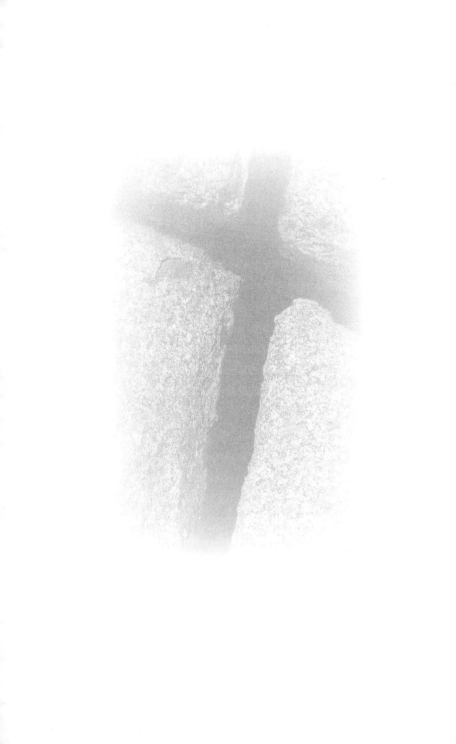

1

Abraham and Isaac

A SPECIAL KIND OF TEST

HAVE YOU EVER RECEIVED mail that isn't addressed to you? You take it out of your mailbox and read that the address doesn't have your name on it. It just says "Occupant." You get that piece of mail by virtue of you being the "occupant" of that home. Trials are a lot like that. Just by virtue of being an occupant on this planet in a fallen world, we will face trials.

Of course, no one likes a trial. No one wakes up in the morning, stretches, and says, "Ah, what a beautiful day for a trial! I think I'd like to have a trial today!" That would be an unusual person who would do something like that. Yet no matter how much we want to avoid trials in our lives, trials are inevitable. No one is immune to trials.

Trials are adverse circumstances that God allows in our lives to both identify where we are spiritually as well as to prepare us for where He wants us to go. There is no escaping them. You are either in a trial now, you've just come out of a trial, or you are getting ready to go into a trial. Trials are unavoidable realities of life.

But even though we all have to experience them, we can take comfort in knowing that trials must first pass through God's hands before reaching us. Nothing comes our way without first having received His divine approval. And in order to get His divine approval, there must be a divine reason for Him to approve it.

There is. God allows trials and tests in our lives in order to reveal where we are along our spiritual journey, to correct us when necessary, and to strengthen us for the journey ahead.

PULLING OUT THE TRICK BAG

A good friend of mine is an assistant football coach for the University of Texas, and he'll call me during all hours of the day or night when he's facing one of these trials. He calls me to talk through his trial, or as he puts it, the "trick bag." In fact, he calls me so much about his "trick bags" that I've now nicknamed my friend "Trick bag," and I call him that every time I see him.

A trick bag is a catch-22. It's where you find yourself stuck between a rock and a hard place. Your back is up against the wall, and no matter how hard you try, there seems to be no visible solution. The only way to get out of your scenario would be illegitimately, because there is no valid way out.

When you are in a trick bag, you feel trapped, stuck, and tired of where you are. You either don't know what to do, or you don't know how to legitimately do what you feel you need to do. You are like Israel when they faced Pharaoh on one side and the Red Sea on the other, and certain death was upon them.

A trick bag is a lose-lose deal. If it were a clear win-lose deal, then you would know how to choose and where to turn. But what do you do when you're caught between a rock and a hard place? What option do you choose when both options are bad? Have you ever been in a situation where all of the ways that you turn to are problems, and you are just trying to find the least possible problem to choose as the solution?

I've been in situations like that and it's not fun. It's about as fun as huffing and puffing on that treadmill in my doctor's office during my annual physical exam. But one thing I've learned over the years is that God has a purpose for these times in our lives. Just like my doctor is not a mean man for putting my body through all of that stress, God is not a mean God when He decrees that we go through trials.

When God wants to reveal the real condition of your heart to empower you toward His plan for your future, He puts you in one of these kinds of trials. And when God puts you in a certain kind of trial, trick bag, catch-22, or between a rock and a hard place, He is getting ready to do something significant in your life. That's the conclusion of this book, and it comes at the beginning.

This is not the typical trial that is used to develop character and reveal flaws. This trick bag signifies that there is accelerated activity about to take place in your situation.

GOD'S BLESSING THROUGH ABRAHAM

The first trick bag that we're going to look at appears in Genesis 22. It's part of the story of Abraham and his son Isaac. Earlier God had made a covenant with Abraham—theologians call this binding agreement the Abrahamic covenant. Through this covenant, God promised that He would bless Abraham and that

Abraham would also be a blessing to others.

Notice that God's covenant didn't stop at His blessing for Abraham. Rather, God's covenant went on to declare that others would be blessed through Abraham. A blessing in the Bible means to experience, enjoy, and extend the favor of God in your life.

Sometimes I get the impression that when we ask God to bless us, we forget the full definition of a blessing. We forget that God doesn't want us to be cul-de-sac Christians where all of our blessings end with us. God wants us to be a conduit Christian where all of our blessings extend through us to others.

God said clearly to Abraham, "Look toward the heavens, and count the stars. . . . So shall your descendants be. . . . In you, all the families of the earth will be blessed" (Genesis 15:5; 12:3).

God said that He was not only going to bring His favor on Abraham but that His favor on Abraham would extend out to be a blessing on others as well. God never designs our blessings to stop with us, but our blessings should always extend to others.

GOD'S MIRACLE FOR ABRAHAM AND SARAH

God's covenant with Abraham would require a miracle just to get it going. Not only were Abraham and his wife, Sarah, advanced in years when God made the promise concerning his descendants, but it would be another twenty-five years before that promise was realized. So here we have an equation that starts with "old" and then adds twenty-five years to it.

By the time Sarah was told she would have a son, both Abraham and she were not only old but also starting to get cold. The early nineties[1] is not typically considered to be the prime time of the married life, if you know what I mean. Even Sarah herself had a difficult time believing God's promise. "Sarah laughed to herself, saying 'After I have become old, shall I have pleasure, my lord being old also?'" (Genesis 18:12). In other words, "Shop's closed. This is not going to happen."

But God is not limited by age or energy. That's the beauty of God. He is not limited by what our finite minds can understand or even by what our physical bodies can perform. And just as God had promised, Isaac was born to Sarah as the seed of Abraham's loins.

GOD'S AMAZING REQUEST OF ABRAHAM

A number of years later, God spoke to Abraham about his son. He did more than just speak to him, though. It actually says in Genesis 22 that God "tested" Abraham. God decided to put Abraham between a rock and a hard place—in a trick bag. He put him in a catch-22. We read:

> Now it came about after these things, that God tested Abraham, and said to him, "Abraham!" And he said, "Here I am." He said, "Take now your son, your only son, whom you love, Isaac, and go to the land of Moriah, and offer him there as a burnt offering on one of the mountains of which I will tell you." (vv. 1–2)

Hold up. We didn't just read that, did we? God didn't just ask Abraham to take his only son, the son whom he loves—the son of God's promise—and go kill him, did he? That's a pretty harsh request to ask someone to do. That's sticking Abraham, the man who followed God in faith all of those years, between a rock and a hard place.

God *did* ask Abraham. And now our brother Abe finds himself in the middle of a contradiction. In fact, Abraham is caught in a slew of contradictions.

Let me explain what I mean. The first kind of contradiction Abraham is in is a theological one. Get this: God had promised Abraham a son. God had said, in essence, "Abraham, I'm going to make your name great. I'm going to give you a son. He's going to have sons. They will have sons. And you will become a great nation." That was a promise. Take it to the bank. It was a promise from God.

Then, however, a few years later God says, in essence, "Abraham, kill that son."

I've seen a few tricky situations in my life but Abraham's trick bag tops them all. Because Abraham is now asking God, "How can my son Isaac become a great nation—as you promised me, God, if I kill him? He's young. He's not even married. He doesn't have any children. And you want me to kill him?"

To which God nods His head, yes.

WOULD GOD PLAY A TRICK ON YOU?

But this book isn't just about Abraham, although Abraham's story is an amazing backdrop on which to see God more clearly. This book is more personal; so for a moment let's bring our focus into the present. What about you? Have you ever felt like God is playing a trick on you? Have you ever felt like God isn't giving you any real options, like you are stuck between a rock and a hard place? Maybe God has given you something that you thought He had promised you, and then just as soon as He gave it to you, He asked you to give it back. Something you waited, prayed, and longed for sincerely. Something good, even spiritual.

It finally showed up in your life and then in your excitement, God said, "Okay, now give it back. Let it go." He asked that we return it . . . or kill it.

When God does something like that, it is only because there is something greater on the other side of His request. But when we are in the middle of the contradictions, it is easy to forget that. Especially when there are multiple contradictions like with Abraham.

DID GOD CONTRADICT GOD?

Not only was it a trick bag for Abraham theologically because it contradicted something God had promised, but it was a trick bag theologically because it contradicted something God had previously said not to do. How could God, who said in Genesis 9:6, "Whoever sheds man's blood, by man his blood shall be shed, for in the image of God He made man" now ask Abraham a mere thirteen chapters later to shed his son's blood? God seemingly contradicted His own request. God contradicted God. When God contradicts God—what do you do? That's a trick bag. (Did God really contradict God when he asked Abraham to sacrifice his son? We will answer this theological and ethical question in chapter 2.)

Have you ever been in a situation where it seems like what God told you in your yesterday contradicts what He is telling you in your today? Has God ever completely confused you, even though you thought you had heard Him correctly both times? I know I have been in situations like that. When this type of trial happens, it is good to remember Abraham.

Because not only were there theological contradictions facing Abraham, but there was also an emotional contradiction. God was asking Abraham to sacrifice his son, whom he loves. "He said, 'Take now your son, your only son, whom you love . . .'" (Genesis 22:2). I can only imagine that God included this personal information in this verse saying, "whom you love" because He wanted us to know that this son was extra special to Abraham.

This trial is a matter of the heart for Abraham. This request cuts deeply into the tenderest part of Abraham's own love. This is God saying, "I know how you feel about your son Isaac, Abraham. I know that you love him more than anything else on earth because he is your only son from Sarah. Not only is he your only son from Sarah, but he is also the son of promise—the son of your future. I know all of this, Abraham. In fact, it is because I know all of this that I want you to give him back."

Sure, there is another son, Ishmael (see Genesis 16). But Abraham doesn't love Ishmael the same way that he loves Isaac, because Isaac is the son of the promise. Isaac came from the womb of Sarah. Ishmael did not.

God says to Abraham, in essence, "I want the one you are really connected to and invested in. Sacrifice him, Abraham. Give him back, Abraham. Take the knife to him, Abraham."

Abraham is facing an emotional contradiction, a trick bag.

MORE CONTRADICTIONS

Not only do we have theological contradictions and an emotional contradiction, but Abraham also experiences social and familial contradictions. What is he going to tell Sarah? What about the neighbors? What are people going to say as they gather every morning around the well and fill up their jugs? Are they going to whisper, "Hey, did you hear that Abraham killed the son of his promise?" Are they going to say that Abraham lost his mind and sabotaged his own future? That is how it would have looked from their vantage point.

Abraham is in conflict on all sides, and not because of any sin that he had committed. He is in conflict because of God.

"Your son, Abraham, your only son whom you love—I want him," God says. "Sacrifice him."

And guess where God is asking him to sacrifice his son Isaac? On the altar. Back in the Bible days, the altar was like church. It was the place to worship through sacrifice.

It's nice to worship God when you're getting everything that you want and all of your prayers are being answered, but what about those times when He's asking you to give up what you want the most? Do you still go to church then? Do you still go to the altar?

DO WE SURRENDER ALL?

What about those times when God asks you to give back to Him what you once told him was His to have. According to Genesis 21:4, Abraham had circumcised Isaac. Circumcision was a sign of the covenant because the covenant was designed to be passed on through the family via the man. The male was circumcised to signify that he was passing on the program of God. So what Abraham had said to God when he circumcised Isaac was that he was committing Isaac to God.

It's one thing to say, "All I have is yours, God." It's another thing to mean it. As long as God is not asking us to give up what is dear to us, we're quick to say that we surrender all. But as soon as God wants it, we can become very territorial, protecting what we once had committed to Him.

Nearly everyone reading this book has been territorial toward God at one time or another. I'm guessing at some point you have found yourself in a spiritual conflict with God. You knew that God wanted you to give up something that seemed legitimate. God wanted you to turn over something that you thought He had given you to begin with: a dream, a relationship, a desire, an ambition, a job, a family member, health, finances, or home. You knew that God was asking you to sacrifice something on His altar, but you also knew how you felt about that sacrifice and how you felt about letting it go.

And it hurt.

God doesn't always ask us to sacrifice something as literal as what we are seeing with Abraham and his son. But He does test our hearts. And it does hurt. Maybe it's not our son that He's asking for. Maybe He's asking for us to remain single longer than we had hoped, or even married longer than we desire. Maybe He's asking us to put our career on the altar, a promotion, a dream, or even a relationship. Whatever it is, God knows how to pick the very thing that will test the deepest parts of our heart.

God does this because He knows that our words alone mean very little. Just like my doctor would be a fool to take my word for how I feel every summer when I visit him, God knows that our words are superficial at best, even with good intentions. Faith only gets tested when our feet move.

ABRAHAM TAKES ACTION

So how do Abraham's feet respond in the situation of a trick bag? They respond in an uncommon way. When we read Genesis 22:3, we see a verse jam-packed with action verbs: "So Abraham rose early in the morning and saddled his donkey, and took two of his young men with him and Isaac his son; and he split wood for the burnt offering, and arose and went to the place of which God had told him."

Notice these words: *rose, saddled, took, split, arose,* and *went*. These are all verbs indicating an immediate response. But also notice what verse 3 doesn't say. It doesn't tell us that Abraham is trying to bargain with God. It doesn't say that Abraham is asking God "Why?" It doesn't say that Abraham snuck a lamb in his backpack, just in case. It doesn't give us a synopsis of a debate going on. No, it just says that Abraham got up, got going, and did what God had asked him to do.

Where did Abraham find not only the strength but also the faith to follow God so quickly on such a seemingly absurd request? The question applies to us as well: Where do we find the strength and the faith to follow God when God puts us in a trick bag?

The answer comes from Abraham's own words. In verse 5 we read, "Abraham said to his young men, 'Stay here with the donkey, and I and the lad will go over there; and we will worship and return to you.'"

Let me break it down for you. Abraham said, "Hey, boys, the son and I are going to go have some church. We're going to go up and worship and then we'll be back."

But wait a minute. Isn't that different than what God had said? God had said to take his son up to the altar and kill him. But Abraham said to the young men that he and his son were going to go to the altar, worship God, and then come back. How could Abraham have said that?

The only way Abraham could have said that was because he fully knew the power of God. Even if Abraham killed his son, Abraham knew that the God he served had promised to bless his son and his son's seed. Therefore, since that promise is true and God does not lie, Abraham knew that if he killed his son, the God he served was powerful enough to keep His promise, even if he didn't understand how.

What Abraham knew—and what you and I know—about God

determine how we respond to God when we are stuck between a rock and a hard place. That is why it is essential to know God in the good times, and to know Him well. Knowing God in times of peace is critical for helping to handle problems in the bad times. Because when you don't know God, or when you either forget or dismiss what is true about Him, then you don't know how to respond when He puts you in a trick bag.

FAITH IN THE ONE YOU BELIEVE IN

We often confuse the essence of faith. Faith is not about how much you believe. In fact, you can have all the faith in the world that your SUV is going to take off and fly you to Canada cruising at 12,000 feet in the air. But that won't change the fact that you're still going to be stuck in traffic somewhere with all four wheels firmly on the ground.

Faith is about believing that the One you believe in is believable.

The way you find out if the one you believe in is believable is by knowing and experiencing Him.

It's like when a child climbs up on the back of her daddy for a piggyback ride. She doesn't get up there and start asking herself if he can hold her or if he is going to drop her. Instead, she immediately starts asking him, "Do you have me? Do you have me?" as she wiggles and adjusts her legs into place.

By asking her daddy, "Do you have me?" she is affirming in her mind that the one she is putting her faith in is faithful. Because if he says, "Yes, I have you," and she rests up there and discovers that he really does have her, then the next time she climbs on for a piggy-back ride, the questions become fewer. Enough piggyback rides later, and she doesn't even ask anymore. In fact, he can toss her up in the air or spin her around in circles and instead of sheer terror, she giggles with excitement because she has faith that the one she believes in is believable.

But until she first climbs up onto the back of her daddy, she can say all day long that she believes that he can hold her. Saying it a thousand times won't reduce the hesitation she feels when the offer to get up there is first extended. She will never get to the point where she can experience the full pleasure of his presence until she takes that first climb of faith to discover that he is faithful.

Faith experienced is faith that is real. Faith cannot be experienced without our feet doing what we say we believe. It is an easy thing to say that you believe. It is an easy thing to feel like you believe. But faith is not situated in our feelings. Faith is situated in our feet. That's why the Bible says "we walk by faith" (see 2 Corinthians 5:7) rather than "feel by faith."

In other words, faith is validated by the steps you take; not by the butterflies that you feel. In fact, you can feel absolutely faithless and yet be entirely full of faith. Or you can feel absolutely faith-full and yet be entirely devoid of faith because your feet are not moving when God says to get up and go.

FAITH SHOWN BY OUR FEET

The measure of a person's faith is in his feet just like the measure of the health of my heart only comes on the treadmill once a year at my doctor's office. The strength of my heart during my medical exam is not determined by my words. Just like Abraham, the strength of our faith is not determined by our words, thoughts, or feelings.

Not until faith registers through actions will we know how much faith we really have. Sometimes it takes a trick bag, or getting caught between a rock and a hard place, to give us an opportunity to put feet on our faith.

Abraham found himself in exactly that position. We'll uncover more about Abraham's faith, as well as God's uncommon response, as we move into the next chapter.

NOTE

1. Sarah was ninety years old and Abraham was ninety-nine when God announced Sarah would bear a son (Genesis 17:1, 16–17).

IN THE HARD PLACES

1. The college football coach calls a situation with no way out a "trick bag." Why do Christians often get upset when they find themselves in a trick-bag situation?

2. Think of a trial when you felt there was no way out, when you felt you were caught between a rock and a hard place. How did you feel about the situation? What were your feelings and thoughts toward God?

3. Early in the chapter Pastor Evans says God allows adverse circumstances in our lives "to both identify where we are spiritually as well as to prepare us for where He wants us to go." He then adds that no trial "comes our way without first having received His divine approval." Do you believe those two statements? If so, what comfort do these statements give you?

4. Merriam-Webster's Collegiate Dictionary defines a catch-22 as "an illogical, unreasonable, or senseless situation." What were a couple of the senseless situations Abraham faced when God told him to kill his son Isaac?

5. Read the entire story in Genesis 22. There is no record in the story that Abraham asked the question "Why?" Are you at the point where if God asked you to do something illogical, you would—without asking why?

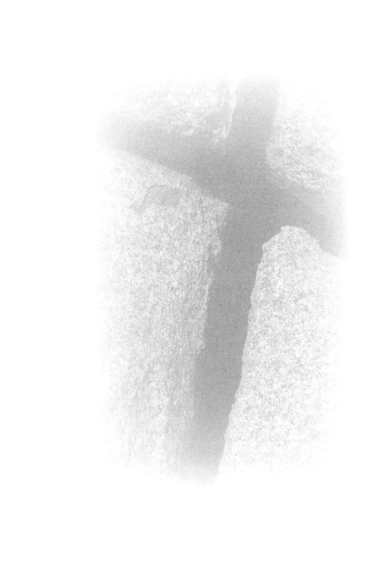

2

Abraham and Isaac

OBEY . . . AND SEE GOD IN A NEW WAY

EARLY IN MY MINISTRY as a pastor I found myself caught between a rock and a hard place, a contradictory situation. Of course, God was getting ready to reveal Himself in an extraordinary way. But when you are caught between a rock and a hard place, that's the first thing you forget.

The church that I continue to pastor today has more than 8,000 members, but it began much, much smaller—just ten individuals coming together. After about a year of gathering in our home, we had grown to about two hundred members who met weekly at a nearby public school. This was back in the day when issues regarding the separation of church and state were just coming to the forefront of public debate and discussion. A number of schools were trying to get God out of their schools in all ways possible.

Eventually school board members told us that we had to move out of the school in which we were meeting. They gave us thirty days to find a new venue. Locating a place to hold a couple of hundred of people on a shoestring budget in Texas proved to be a challenge, as you might have guessed. We searched high and low for a place but nothing turned up. Before we knew it, we were nearing the end of our thirty-day notice. We still didn't have anywhere to go.

Knowing that two hundred people were way too many to meet in our small home, we drafted a letter and sent it to the school board asking for an extension. About as fast as you can read this sentence, we got a letter back saying that no extension would be granted because, as they said, the majority of the school board was against it.

AWAITING THE FINAL DECISION

However, they also said that they would need to hold an official vote on that decision at their next scheduled meeting. This meeting just so happened to be a few days prior to our last Sunday at the school.

Talk about having my back up against a wall. With nowhere to go, no money to go there with, and no options before us, we were in a trick bag.

God had called me to start this church. He had confirmed that to my wife, Lois, and me through a number of ways, and we had no doubt about His calling. But here we were facing a situation that meant closing our doors in less than a week's time. What now?

Not knowing exactly what to do, we did the only thing that we could do: call on God to intervene. We decided to go to the scheduled school board meeting ourselves and sit outside their conference room while they met. The school board was going to have to give us this news to our faces.

I, along with my associate pastor, drove to the school and we sat there together waiting for them to hand out their decision. The meeting had been scheduled for 2 o'clock; time passed, and it was now 2:30. We hadn't heard anything on what was supposed to be a fairly quick and easy vote. Soon we looked at our watches and it was 3:00. Then it was 3:30, and still nothing. We kept waiting.

Finally, one of the school board members came out and looked at both of us, seeing the anticipation all over our faces. She said, "We can't quite figure this out, but the two main people who are against you have not gotten to the meeting yet."

My associate pastor and I turned to look at each other, and then we turned to look back at the school board member, who continued.

"They are not here, and we can't wait on them any longer. So we went ahead and voted with the members who are here, and I've come out to let you know that your extension has been granted by a vote of 4–3."

What happened next was even more amazing. No kidding, at the very moment she told us this news, the two missing board members came rushing in the front door, huffing and puffing and out of breath.

"We're sorry we're late," one of them told her. "There was an accident on the highway at our exit."

Come to find out the two board members who were our strongest opponents were riding to the meeting together. But instead of making it to the meeting on time, they got stuck in traffic for an hour and a half and entirely missed the vote. I will never forget that day or the looks on those two board members' faces when they heard that the vote had already happened. God allowed our church to be caught between a rock and a hard place, where there were no good options for us to even choose, so that we could learn something about Him. (I'll describe the final outcome in the beginning of chapter 3.)

I thought my school board problem was a big one. I wonder how Abraham felt when he was asked to take a knife to the very fulfillment of his promise.

ISAAC'S INNOCENT QUESTION

As Abraham and Isaac neared the place of the altar, Isaac's curiosity got the best of him, and he questioned his dad about this whole "worship" experience. In Genesis 22:7, we read, "Isaac spoke to Abraham his father and said, 'My father!' And he said, 'Here I am, my son.' And he said, 'Behold, the fire and the wood, but where is the lamb for the burnt offering?'"

It was an innocent-enough question. There they were, trekking up a pretty steep mountain, carrying a cumbersome load of wood, and Isaac probably just wanted to make sure that when they got there, they were not going to have to turn around and do it all over again.

ABRAHAM'S SIMPLE ANSWER

The response came in verse 8. "Abraham said, 'God will provide for Himself the lamb for the burnt offering, my son.' So the two of them walked on together."

When you are caught in a trick bag, you really don't have any solid answers, do you? That's why it's a trick bag. You don't know how things are going to work out. Just like we could have never predicted that there would have been an accident on the highway the day that the school board was scheduled to meet, Abraham didn't know how God was going to get him out of this one. So he just kept going, all the while telling Isaac, "Son, God's got to answer your question. God's got to provide the solution to this problem because I don't have one. Only God can fix this. God will provide." Abraham's answer to Isaac's question was simple and true: "God will provide."

Father and son kept walking. Eventually, Abraham got to the point where he had to make his ultimate decision. "Then they came to the place of which God had told him; and Abraham built the altar there and arranged the wood, and bound his son Isaac and laid him on the altar, on top of the wood" (v. 9).

How I would have loved to have been a bug in the sand at this point in the story just to see Isaac's response as his father tied him up and laid him on top of the wood—and the expression on Abraham's face. Perhaps Abraham's chest heaved from the labored breathing and the deep sighs from both the long walk up the mountain and the utter confusion in the whole situation.

THE DECISIVE MOMENT

We read about this decisive moment in verse 10: "Abraham stretched out his hand and took the knife to slay his son."

This is where the progression of the story comes to an abrupt halt. Right when Abraham takes the knife to slay his son, the Angel of the Lord calls to him. The passage reads:

> But the angel of the Lord called to him from heaven and said, "Abraham, Abraham!" And he said, "Here I am." He said, "Do not stretch out your hand against the lad, and do nothing to him; for

now I know that you fear God, since you have not withheld your son, your only son, from Me." (vv. 11–12)

Hold up. Don't we have a problem? Abraham is picking up the knife to radically obey God. He's ready to slay his son when the Angel of the Lord, who is Jesus Christ preincarnate—a member of the triune Godhead—stops him and says not to kill Isaac. And that's good. Up until then, we're still doing great. Super, don't kill the boy. Thank you, Jesus!

THE ZINGER

But here comes the zinger, when He throws in a line that is a theological conundrum. It goes like this:

"Now I know that you fear God."

This is one of those times in the Bible where an omniscient God who knows everything speaks to a man about something that He just came to know. That's another contradiction right there, because how can God know everything but only now come to know something? That is the apparent indication of that phrase, but also a seemingly obvious contradiction of the omniscience of God.

David highlighted God's omniscience when he wrote,

O Lord, You have searched me and known me. You know when I sit down and when I rise up; You understand my thought from afar. You scrutinize my path and my lying down, and are intimately acquainted with all my ways. Even before there is a word on my tongue, Behold, O Lord, You know it all. (Psalm 139:1–4)

God knows everything that ever was, is, or will be. Not only does God know everything actual, but God also knows everything potential. He not only knows what is; He knows what could have been or can be. In the New Testament, we find Jesus making this statement, "Woe to you, Chorazin! Woe to you, Bethsaida! For if the miracles had occurred in Tyre and Sidon which occurred in you, they would have repented long ago in sackcloth and ashes" (Matthew 11:21). In those words, Jesus was letting them know what He knew about what could have been.

WHAT GOD KNOWS

Yet while God knows everything actual and potential, we need to remember that God does not necessarily know everything experiential. Now wait, before you close this book and run off to send me a long, heated e-mail about what I just said, track with me a bit. For example, what if I were to ask you, "Does God know how it feels to commit a sin?" I would suggest to you that He couldn't tell you how it would feel for Him to commit a sin because He has never experienced committing a sin. When Jesus bore our sin on the cross, He bore *our* sin. God has never had the experience of committing a sin.

Does God know what sin is? Absolutely. God knows all there is to know information-wise about sin, except for the doing of it. Because He's never done it. So when the Angel of the Lord says to Abraham, "Now I know . . . ", He's not talking about informational knowledge. God is omniscient with regard to information. What God is saying to Abraham is, "Now I have experienced that you fear Me."

God is a God of information and knowledge, but God is also a God of experience. He enters into our emotions, to use human terminology. And so He listens in to our praise. Why doesn't He just sit back, relax, and say, "I know what praise is. I have all of the information on praise available to me. In fact, I know who is going to praise me, who is praising me now, and who has praised me in the past—what's more, I know who means it. I don't need anyone to praise Me since I already know everything there is to know about praise." Yet the Bible tells us that God is enthroned upon the praises offered to Him (see Psalm 22:3). To be enthroned on something is to be in the midst of it, a participant in it. God purposefully and willingly participates in the experience.

Why did God become a man? Not only to redeem us from a life of eternal punishment and separation, but also to participate in the human experience. Because it is through Jesus Christ becoming a man that He is now able to sympathize with us. The writer of Hebrews tells us, "For we do not have a high priest who cannot sympathize with our weaknesses, but One who has been tempted in all things as we are, yet without sin" (Hebrews 4:15). Jesus can sympathize with us because He has gone through everything that a person goes through, except for sin.

So when the Angel of the Lord says, "Now I know that you fear God," it is because He has now taken part in experiential participation. God enters into that moment in time when He experiences and feels the love that we sing, speak, and think about.

"You say that you'll give me your son?" God asks Abraham. "Now I know. I know it experientially. You chose Me over what you love more than anything else in the world."

One reason God puts you and me between a rock and a hard place is to give us that opportunity to enter into a relational experience with Him. He puts us in a trick bag so that He can ask us to give up our own "Isaac."

What is your "Isaac?" It is anything that you love, treasure, or value most. God desires that we esteem Him above the most valued thing in our lives. This is when the abundant life comes, when we experience a side of God that very few people ever know. We discover things about God that others never get to enjoy, just like Abraham did.

A PATIENT GOD WAITS

In Abraham's situation, God does not make His move to reveal His provision until after Abraham obeyed Him. Second Peter 3:9 tells us, "The Lord is not slow about His promise, as some count slowness, but is patient toward you, not wishing for any to perish but for all to come to repentance." God has already made His promise, but we also read here that He is waiting in patience for a response from us before He fulfills this promise.

Some things God initiates in His sovereignty simply because He has chosen to. But there are many things, and I would daresay the majority of things, that He does which are tied to what we do.

We see this a number of times in the Mosaic covenant when God says, "If you do this, then I'm going to do this." Or, "If you don't do this, then I'm going to do this." God often waits to see what we will do and then responds according to His character. Realizing this key theological truth can be life changing. It is one of the most important principles that you can ever learn. It removes the issue of obedience out of a category of "rules" and places it into a category of "relational participation." Obedience frees God up to respond in the way that He promised He would do.

Understanding obedience through those eyes makes it come alive to me because now I am not just following a list of dos and don'ts. Now I am entering into a covenantal relationship with a God who cannot lie and who will keep His end of the agreement when I reveal to Him, through my feet, that I believe He will do that. Now I am actually setting the stage for the movement of God in my circumstances, relationships, job, home, or life. I am doing that just like Abraham did when he picked up the knife to slay the son of his promise.

What happened after the Angel of the Lord spoke to Abraham? We read on:

> Then Abraham raised his eyes and looked, and behold, behind him a ram caught in the thicket by his horns; and Abraham went and took the ram and offered him up for a burnt offering in the place of his son. Abraham called the name of that place The Lord Will Provide, as it is said to this day, "In the mount of the Lord it will be provided." (Genesis 22:13–14)

Little did Abraham know that all the while he was hiking up one side of the mountain, God was bringing his solution up the other side of the mountain. While Abraham climbed up the steep path, the ram also climbed up the other side. But Abraham couldn't have known that ahead of time because God is not going to reveal what He's up to until obedience has been completed.

God didn't show Abraham anything until Abraham took the knife to slay his son. Abraham arising early in the morning wasn't enough. Abraham chopping the firewood wasn't enough. Abraham climbing the mountain wasn't enough.

God showed Abraham the ram when Abraham did what God had said. He will do the same thing for us when we do what He has asked us to do.

If you ever find yourself stuck between a rock and a hard place, or if you are there right now, remember that going halfway through obedience won't cut it. The obedience that God wants must be completed before you will get to experience the abundance of knowing God as your Provider firsthand.

SEEING GOD IN A NEW WAY

God didn't just give Abraham a ram; He gave him much more. We read in the next few verses:

> Then the angel of the Lord called to Abraham a second time from heaven, and said, "By Myself I have sworn, declares the Lord, because you have done this thing and have not withheld your son, your only son, indeed I will greatly bless you, and I will greatly multiply your seed as the stars of the heavens and as the sand which is on the seashore; and your seed shall possess the gate of their enemies. In your seed all the nations of the earth shall be blessed, because you have obeyed My voice." (Genesis 22:15–18)

Do you hear what God is saying? "Because you did not withhold the thing that I had asked you for, Abraham, which was the most valued thing in your life; indeed, I will greatly bless you," God promises. "Because you have obeyed Me, you now get to see Me in a new way."

Several thousand years later the writer of Hebrews emphasized this promise to the followers of Jesus:

> When God made the promise to Abraham, since He could swear by no one greater, He swore by Himself, saying, "I will surely bless you and I will surely multiply you." And so, having patiently waited, he obtained the promise. For men swear by one greater than themselves, and with them an oath given as confirmation is an end of every dispute. In the same way God, desiring even more to show to the heirs of the promise the unchangeableness of His purpose, interposed with an oath, so that by two unchangeable things in which it is impossible for God to lie, we who have

taken refuge would have strong encouragement to take hold of the hope set before us. (Hebrews 6:13–18)

GOD IS UNCHANGEABLE

The writer of Hebrews tells us about an Old Testament story to make a New Testament point—God is unchangeable. He mentions "two unchangeable things in which it is impossible for God to lie."

What are these two unchangeable things? They are God's promise and His oath.

Twenty-five years before Sarah would even conceive his son, God made a promise to Abraham: "I will make you a great nation . . . and so you shall be a blessing" (Genesis 12:2). But Abraham still had to wait twenty-five years.

A promise will happen but it often requires waiting. There is a difference between a promise and an oath. An oath is given when it is time for it to happen, while a promise doesn't always have time associated with it. We've all experienced this. We've read in the Bible about God's promises and have quoted that they are "Yes, and amen." But we still sit around waiting for them to happen.

Yet when God is ready to give an oath, He is ready to take action. Look at Abraham's example. In chapter 2 of Genesis, God gave him a promise. God repeated that promise in chapter 15, and then again in chapter 17. But in chapter 22, God says to Abraham, "Now I swear to you."

That's an oath.

Here is the beauty of an oath. When God makes an oath, there is nothing left for you to do. The wait is over.

The twenty-five years that Abraham had to wait to receive the promise of his son was time that God used to develop in him the kind of faith that would take him up the side of a mountain when God would later ask him to do that. Because if you think back to Abraham and how he was early on, he was—what we would call it where I come from—a punk.

Abraham lied about his wife only telling that she was his sister because he was afraid that someone might beat him up, or even kill him (Genesis 20). He got impatient about God's promise of a child, so he went ahead and made a baby with his handmaiden instead (Genesis 16).

God knew that Abraham had issues, so God made a promise to Abraham early on in anticipation of Abraham one day pushing past his issues. When God saw that Abraham's faith had reached that place, He made an oath.

Not only did God make an oath with Abraham at that time, but when we look at James' account of the story in the New Testament, we discover that Abraham got even more.

James asks his readers, "What use is it, my brethren, if someone says he has faith but has no works? Can that faith save him?" (James 2:14). We know that he's not talking about eternal salvation, because he's addressing a group of people who are already on their way to heaven. He has called them "my brethren."

The salvation James is referring to is the same salvation he references in chapter 1 when he writes, "Therefore, putting aside all filthiness and all that remains of wickedness, in humility receive the word implanted, which is able to save your souls" (1:21). James is talking about a life transformation that happens as the Word of God sanctifies our souls.

Now in James 2:15–16, the apostle distinguishes between a useful and a useless faith. He writes, "If a brother or sister is without clothing and in need of daily food, and one of you says to them,

'Go in peace, be warmed and be filled,' and yet you do not give them what is necessary for their body, what use is that?"

All of us have faith to some degree, but we do not all have a useful faith. James describes useless faith even further, "Even so faith, if it has no works, is dead, being by itself" (v. 17).

Later, James illustrates his point through the life of Abraham:

> Was not Abraham our father justified by works when he offered up Isaac his son on the altar? You see that faith was working with his works, and as a result of the works, faith was perfected; and the Scripture was fulfilled which says, "And Abraham believed God, and it was reckoned to him as righteousness," and he was called the friend of God. (vv. 21–23)

BEING A FRIEND OF GOD

Did you catch that? Abraham got more than a promise. Abraham got more than an oath. Abraham got God Himself calling him His own friend. When did Abraham become known as a friend of God? When he acted in faith on the command of God. Abraham was brought into an inner circle of a unique group of people with God. I can't think of anything I would like to be known for more than being a friend of God.

One way that you and I can be called a friend of God is to follow the example of Abraham, especially when he was caught between a rock and a hard place. Do you remember Abraham's initial response when he was told to take his son up the mountain to sacrifice him? "So Abraham rose early in the morning . . . " (Genesis 22:3).

It's easy to miss, but those seven small words are loaded with impact and meaning. Because when Abraham was caught between a rock and a hard place, those seven words reveal that he did not even hesitate. Abraham got up early to move head-on toward what seemed like ultimate disaster.

The reason Abraham didn't hesitate is given to us in a key New Testament reference to this story found in Hebrews chapter 11:

> By faith Abraham, when he was tested, offered up Isaac, and he who had received the promises was offering up his only begotten son; it was he to whom it was said, "In Isaac your descendants shall be called." He considered that God is able to raise people even from the dead, from which he also received him back as a type. (vv. 17–19)

Remember that inexplainable contradiction of God calling for the death of Abraham's son? God, who acts according to His character, is the death conqueror, and *Abraham believed this*. (In addition, God asked Abraham to sacrifice, not murder, his son. In hindsight, we see God planned to give the ram as a substitution.)

Abraham believed that even if he killed Isaac, God had the power to raise him from the dead. Abraham knew that God couldn't lie. And if God can't lie, then Abraham knew that God was not finished with Isaac's life. He banked on the fact that the God whom He couldn't understand had power to overrule the confusion. He banked on the omnipotence of God even when He didn't grasp omniscience. He banked everything on the faithfulness of God even when it didn't make sense.

Let me explain something about God: He is the inexplicable God. He is the unfigure-outable God. His ways are not our ways. His thoughts are not our thoughts. He has a million ways to hit a bull's-eye with a crooked stick.

Don't waste your time trying to figure out *how* He's going to do it. Don't waste your time trying to figure out *when* He's going to do it. Don't waste your time trying to figure out *where* He's going to do it. Don't waste your time because you'll never figure out God. He's not going to tell you until it is the time for Him to do it. The reason He's not going to tell you is because He wants you to discover Him, and He wants to experience you—on a whole new level.

After the knife and the ram, Abraham is not just Abraham any longer. Abraham is a friend of God. Because Abraham is a friend of God, his blessings extend beyond himself to others as we read earlier, "he also received him back as a type."

What is a "type?" A type is something physical that represents something greater spiritually. For example, the sacrifices performed in the Old Testament were a type of Christ and His sacrifice.

So when we read that Abraham got Isaac back not just as a physical reality to a physical father but also as a "type," we see a representation of a spiritual principle meant for all of us today. The spiritual principle that I mentioned earlier is this: God is able to supernaturally work in the contradictions of life to bring about things that are inexplicable.

EVEN WITH CONTRADICTIONS, GO FORWARD

All we need to know in the middle of our trick bag is that God is able to not only raise the dead, but to do so much more. When we know this, not just intellectually, we will also rise up early to do what God has said.

Faith must operate in the tensions of life for those who fear God. Even though it was tough, Abraham rose to go and worship God anyway. Even though it was a contradiction, Abraham saddled his donkey to head up the mountain anyway. Even though he found himself between a rock and a hard place, Abraham split the wood that he would put on the altar to obey God anyway. Abraham believed anyway. Abraham acted anyway. Abraham went anyway.

I wonder if any of us have been in a situation where to worship God, or to believe God, or to follow God is connected with an "anyway." Have you ever faced a trial where what you knew the Bible said was not what God seemed to be doing? Have you ever been in a situation where what you knew God had promised was not how God was acting? Have you ever experienced a time when you knew that God told you that He loved you, but it seemed as if He was treating you like He didn't? Yet He still expects you to follow and obey Him even when He makes absolutely no sense at all.

I've been there myself, and I suspect that if you picked up this book, you have been there, know someone who has been there, or you are there now, too.

What I want to remind you as we press on together through the stories of the lives of other men and women in the remaining chapters, is that when God puts you, me, or anyone else between a rock and a hard place—in a trick bag—where there literally seems to be no good way out of the situation, He does this because something significant is about to happen.

But we will never see this significant act of God in our lives if we don't follow Abraham's example to do what God says . . . anyway.

I urge you to step out in the middle of the contradiction, anyway.

Because God is a God who not only raises the dead and makes good on His promises, but He is a God who longs to call you His friend.

IN THE HARD PLACES

---

1. When Isaac asked his father where the lamb for the sacrifice was, what was Abraham's simple answer?

2. How did God provide a way out for Abraham's dilemma? More importantly, *why* did God provide a way out, according to Genesis 22:12?

3. To trust God with our "Isaac"—with anything that we love, treasure, or value most—is a difficult choice, but to choose not to do so is to show we esteem it above God. What is your Isaac? If God asked you to give it up, do you think you could do so?

4. Abraham had to wait twenty-five years for the promise of a son to become reality. During that time God had Abraham deal with at least two issues, impatience and lying (Genesis 16, 20). What issue in your life may explain a rock-and-a-hard place situation you may have experienced—or may be experiencing—in your life?

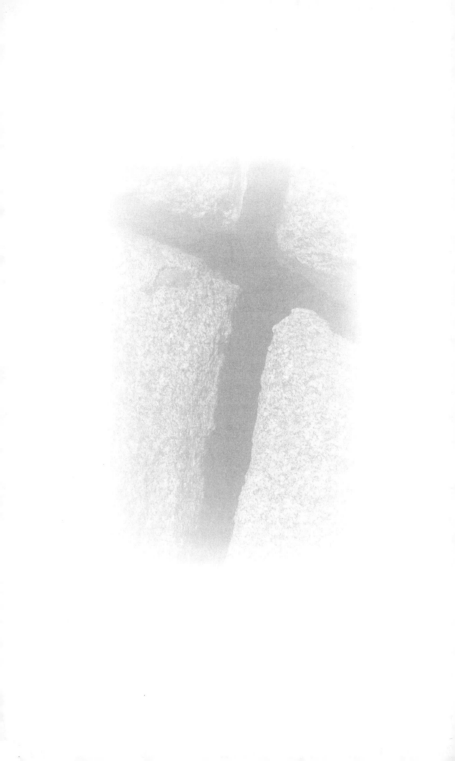

3

Moses and the Israelites

CLAIM YOUR COVENANTAL RIGHTS

REMEMBER HOW GOD intervened after a school board asked us to stop holding church in their school? God stalled our two fiercest opponents from reaching the meeting in time to vote us out.

We received a six-month extension to find another place. Eventually, though, we found ourselves in another trick bag. We had a growing congregation and nowhere to go at the end of our extension.

With the days dwindling, we decided the best scenario would be to purchase our own facility. A handful of us went looking for available property. Shortly after we started, we heard about a tiny A-frame church that might be coming on the market soon. This church held around 250 people. Not only was it located on a major street in our section of Dallas, but it also came with two acres of land.

I discovered that I already knew the pastor of this Bible church and that the members were getting ready to relocate to another piece of property in the suburbs. What I liked most about this little church was its potential. Dozens of untouched acres stretched out all around it. I wasn't thinking so much about the little A-frame building when I saw it, but about the possibilities for expansion. All of those acres of grass and trees sat embedded in the middle of a thriving neighborhood in Dallas. I knew that if we could just get this small chapel, maybe one day we could get all of the land around it, too.

So I went and met with the pastor. I told him that I had heard that they were thinking about moving. He said it was true, and that they were getting ready to put their building up for sale to the public any day. I asked him how much he had hoped to sell it for. He told me two hundred thousand dollars.

He might as well have said two *million* dollars because as a church, we weren't just "poor"—we were, as we call it where I come from, "poh." "Poh" translates into "super poor." We probably had only two thousand dollars in the bank. We didn't own anything. We didn't have any collateral. We didn't even have enough for a down payment. The pastor said that he wanted to sell the church to us, but that he needed the full amount in order to make their move to the suburbs.

But then he added, "Tony, I'll tell you what. We won't put the church on the market for another thirty days in case the Lord wants you to have it. You have thirty days to see if He will come through for you."

As I said earlier, when God puts you, me, or anyone else in between a rock and a hard place, He does so because something significant is about to happen. And this was another rock and a hard place. We were in a trick bag because the church building, location, and property seemed perfect for our vision to reach the Dallas community. But we didn't have the money. We didn't have the time. We had only thirty days to come up with two hundred thousand dollars.

I quickly called some banks to check into getting a loan. They all turned us down. So we prayed, "Lord, if You want us to have this building for the work that You are doing, then we need nothing short of a supernatural intervention on Your part. And we need You to intervene in less than thirty days."

MEET BOB #1 AND BOB #2

A few weeks later, I got an idea to give a call to a friend of mine who was in real estate. I asked Bob if I could come up and meet with him to brainstorm how we might be able to purchase this property, without money or collateral.

Bob agreed to meet. I drove up to his office on the north side of Dallas. We sat down together looking for different options about this church and land. Not long into our brainstorming session, a man whose name is Robert, I'll call him Bob #2, passed by the door. The two Bobs greeted each other, and then Bob #2 walked on.

My friend Bob and I resume discussing the church property. After a while, I notice that the guy who had passed by earlier, the other Bob, is now standing at the door. Bob #1 and I are talking. Bob #2 is standing there while not saying a word. Do you know how annoyed you get when you are trying to carry on a serious conversation with somebody and someone else, whom you didn't invite, gets in your business? Because I'm a preacher, I have extra pressure to try and stay calm, but to me that's irritating.

I'm thinking, *Why is this man all mixed in my Kool-Aid? I didn't invite him. I don't even know him.* But as a preacher I sat there, attempting to be polite.

Then, it went from bad to worse. I'm talking to my friend Bob, and Bob #2 decides to walk in and sit down. My thoughts quickly move from Christian to carnal, as I'm getting royally ticked off. I need to find a way to purchase a two hundred thousand dollar piece of property in two weeks, the banks have turned us down, and we don't have any money. Here is my one opportunity to meet with a real estate specialist for a few minutes to brainstorm possibilities, and this stranger named Bob decides to cut in on our meeting and chat. Come on!

Bob #2 then proceeds to dominate the entire direction of the conversation by asking me a series of questions. I do my best to remain as polite as I can. I answer his questions thoroughly. I find out he is a real estate agent with another company that shares offices with Bob #1's realty company. The two Bobs are friends, of course, and Bob #2 soon tells me he is a Christian attending a local church. But not much more. Just lots of questions.

Those questions turn into a forty-five-minute session. This leaves me no time with my friend Bob at the end of it. We decide to wrap up our meeting because time is now gone.

BOB #2 TAKES ACTION

So there I am, about to grab my belongings, all the while feeling frustrated at what I perceive to have been a wasted meeting. I'm trying not to let any of these emotions show because I want to represent God the way He should be reflected.

Thankfully, I didn't let them show, because then, in the midst of all of these contradicting feelings, Bob #2 does something that I never expected. First, he reaches into his coat pocket and pulls out his checkbook. Next, he writes me a check for the entire amount of two hundred thousand dollars.

Now, I've never seen this man before in my life. Yet, after a forty-five-minute conversation, he writes me a check for the full amount of the purchase price of the property we needed to buy. That's not luck. That's God. That's a God-styled provision of our small A-frame building with two acres.

Today, we own 160 acres of land all around that A-frame chapel. This acreage sits in the middle of a residential Dallas community. If you were to drive down Camp Wisdom Road today, where our church rests, you would see sixty million dollars worth of our church's development since the time Bob #2 wrote out that check.

God had us between a rock and a hard place because He wanted us, and everyone else, to know that He alone was able to get us out of it. Only God can claim the credit for what He has done on Camp Wisdom Road in Dallas, Texas.

Remember, when God has you between a rock and a hard place, He's got something significant coming your way. Don't give up. Hang in there. Keep on pushing through. God allows contradictions to come into the lives of His people in order to take them to a new spiritual level. He allows, and often creates, trick-bag scenarios in order to grant us a new spiritual experience that will give us a bigger view of Him than we previously had.

No, these are not the most pleasant situations when you are in the middle of them. But one thing you can bank on: You are in for something big when God Himself puts you between a rock and a hard place. These situations are intentional, purposeful, and, when responded to appropriately through visible faith, very profitable.

THE BIRTH OF A NATION

Let's build on that lesson by looking at a different kind of trick bag, one held by the people of Israel. In Exodus 2, the Israelites find themselves in a bad situation. Through a series of events (recorded in the book of Genesis), God has birthed a nation—descendants of Abraham, Isaac, and Jacob—in a pagan land called Egypt. There the nation of Israel expands as the twelve sons of Jacob (who has been renamed Israel) develop. Eventually Jacob's descendants are held hostage in Egypt, slaves to Pharaoh.

First, we read they cried out because of their bondage. "Now it came about in the course of those many days that the king of Egypt died. And the sons of Israel sighed because of the bondage, and they cried out; and their cry for help because of their bondage rose up to God" (v. 23).

Have you ever sighed because of your circumstances? You look around you and the most that you can do is just take a deep breath in, and then sigh. Things are not getting any better. Instead of waking up in the morning and saying, "Thank God, another day," you wake up and sigh, "Oh . . . another day."

That's exactly how the nation of Israel felt. Their situation had been bad for so long that all they could do anymore was sigh. Out of their sigh, they cried out to God.

A COVENANT REMEMBERED

And God heard them. "God heard their groaning; and God remembered His covenant with Abraham, Isaac and Jacob" (v.24).

Notice that "God remembered His covenant." A dominant

word from that phrase that we often see throughout the Scriptures is "covenant." Let's take a moment to unpack the spiritual truth associated with a covenant before we go deeper into the story, because it is so influential in many situations. If you can grasp and apply this spiritual truth, then you are well on your way to a dynamic and satisfying earthly existence.

God functions in history not merely on a personal level, but also on a legal level. This legal level is referred to as a "covenant." A covenant is a spiritually binding agreement that God makes with men whereby He agrees to do certain things on their behalf. We often call those things "blessings," based on prescribed terms. A covenant is a legal agreement that God has made with mankind.

FOUR OLD TESTAMENT COVENANTS

We described the Abrahamic covenant in chapter 1. God had made an agreement with Abraham that He was going to bless him in order to make him a blessing to others. The Abrahamic covenant is the covenant that God is remembering in this passage we are looking at in Exodus where it says, "God remembered His covenant."

Later God made a covenant with Moses and the children of Israel, and, later still, with King David. In the Mosaic covenant God said, "If you diligently obey the Lord your God . . . all these blessings will come upon you." God then listed different commands and blessings. And conversely, He said, "If you do not obey the Lord your God . . . all these curses will come upon you" (Deuteronomy 28:1–2, 15). This is also followed by a list. In the Davidic covenant God declared that the eternal King of Israel would come through David's line. We also have the Palestinian covenant, which promised that the land of Palestine would belong to Israel, which is why there's so much conflict today.

OUR COVENANTAL RIGHTS

You and I, as followers of King Jesus, fall under a covenant today—the new covenant. It is described in the Book of Jeremiah: "'Behold, days are coming,' declares the Lord, 'when I will make a new covenant with the house of Israel and with the house of Judah'" (31:31). In this covenant God is referring to the relationship and covering of the Holy Spirit through the blood of Jesus Christ.

The new covenant is spiritually based, made to believers in Christ and based on the sacrificial death, atonement, and resurrection of Jesus Christ. Christians recognize and affirm this new covenant each time they take Communion.

One of the main statements attached to the act of Communion comes from Jesus, who during the Last Supper said, "This cup is the new covenant in My blood; do this, as often as you drink it, in remembrance of Me" (1 Corinthians 11:25; see Luke 22:20). That essential reference to what would become Communion is elaborated on by Paul, who said, "Is not the cup of blessing which we bless a sharing in the blood of Christ?" (1 Corinthians 10:16). The apostle then referred to the bread in the same context. Why did Paul refer to the cup and the bread in the context of blessing? Because God uniquely shows up during the time of Communion to respond to His covenantal agreements.

Communion is not just a time for dim lights, soft music, and closed eyes. When Jesus says, "This cup is the new covenant in My blood; do this . . . in remembrance of Me," He's reminding us to recognize more than what happened two thousand years ago. He's reminding us to consider the implication of what happened at the cross in light of the new covenant for today. But if you don't know and understand the new covenant, then you won't utilize the terms of this new arrangement in the present. You won't get the full benefits of the new covenant because covenants are tied to participation.

The new covenant is tied to our relationship with the Holy Spirit. In the Old Testament, God the Father was front-page news. In the Gospels, God the Son was front-page news. In the church age, God the Spirit is front-page news. We live in the age of the Holy Spirit. That's why if there is not a dynamic relationship with the Holy Spirit, then all of the arrangements God has made through the covenant will not be fully realized because we won't know that they are ours or how they are to be made accessible to us.

Remember Jesus' story of the persistent widow? "A judge who did not fear God and did not respect man" faced a widow who came to him again and again, pleading that he give her legal protection from her opponent. "For a while he was unwilling," Jesus said, "but afterward he said to himself, 'Even though I do not fear God nor respect man, yet because this widow bothers me, I will give her legal protection, otherwise by continually coming she will wear me out'" (Luke 18:2–5).

The widow kept nagging the judge until he relented. But he didn't give in because he liked her. He gave in because her request was persistent. The tendency is to think that to preach, teach, or apply persistence is the sole point of this story. But I don't want us to miss something just as substantial. Twice in this short passage, we read that the widow nagged the judge because of her *legal* rights. She wasn't just nagging him because she wanted something. The widow kept bothering him because she had legal rights that it was his job to enforce.

You and I have legal rights, specifically in heaven. Once you became a son or daughter of God, you entered into a covenant with God that endowed you with certain legal rights. Just like you have constitutional and unalienable rights as an American citizen because you were born here, when you were born again through your relationship with Jesus Christ, you received the new covenant rights. So when Jesus says to "do this in remembrance of Me" as we take Communion, He is not just saying that we should remember that He died, but He's also telling us to remember the rights we have received in relationship to His death through the new covenant.

The Communion table is not just designed to be a spiritual moment where we entertain feelings toward Christ and His sacrifice, although that's included. It is also designed to be a covenantal connection to the legal rights His death secured for you.

When we read earlier about Israel's bondage, we saw that the Israelites cried out to God and in response He remembered His covenant. He remembered His agreement. He remembered their rights. In other words, God was not just responding to their cries and their prayer, He was responding to an obligation that He had made to them. For lack of a better way of putting it, God can be held hostage to His own Word. He can be held hostage to His own Word because He holds Himself hostage to it. That's why you'll often read in the Bible about God changing His mind. How can the God who changes not change His mind? Because God can always adjust to Himself. When He is held accountable to Himself, based on what He has said in His Word through a covenantal agreement, He will respond to that.

PRAYING ACCORDING TO OUR LEGAL RIGHTS

One of the most important things that we can do as Christians is to pray in line with our legal rights. But we often don't do this because we misunderstand what prayer is. Prayer is not simply talking to God. Rather, *prayer is asserting earthly permission for heavenly interference.* Prayer is earth giving heaven authorization to intervene in the affairs of earth as heaven has previously stated that it would. That permission is granted based on your legal position and rights. That's why it is essential to study the Word of God and to know the rights that He has granted you through His Word.

When Israel cried out to God, He remembered His covenant. God engaged the terms of His covenant because of their appeal to Him. This principle can be applied to our lives when we find ourselves caught between a rock and a hard place like Israel. We too can appeal to God. Israel's dilemma centered around a form of bondage. Our bondage might not be the same as it was for the Hebrew slaves. But it can be any kind of stronghold that holds us captive. This might be a stronghold of addiction, food, sex, unhealthy relationship patterns, low self-esteem, materialism, elitism, or any number of things.

Egypt illegitimately held Israel in bondage. Israel cried out to be delivered from that bondage. God heard Israel's cry and responded to them based on His covenantal agreement with them. If you are being held in bondage by an illegitimate force in your life, cry out to God. Pray to God for deliverance by appealing to Him based on your covenantal rights. There is a legal obligation that God has: to respond to you based on the fact that you have a legitimate agreement with Him found in His Word.

Go through the Scriptures and read everything that relates to your stronghold and pray it back to God. When you do that, prayer is no longer just a spiritual exercise or something to check off of your "Christian List of Things To Do." Rather, prayer becomes a legal meeting where you and God get together in agreement on the same covenantal arrangement. Prayer becomes an act of holding God accountable, in the right sense of the word, to what He holds Himself accountable: His Word.

When God heard Israel cry out to Him, He "took notice of them" (Exodus 2:25). While He always knew what was happening, He heard their sigh and their cries and saw them from a covenantal perspective.

CRYING OUT FOR YOUR COVENANTAL RIGHTS

Before we dive further into the story of the Israelite's trial (in our next chapter), let's realize that Israel's slavery is one dramatic form of being caught between a rock and a hard place. The Israelites knew that they legally shouldn't be in the situation that they were in, slaves to the Egyptians. They wanted out. They just didn't know how to get out. The thing that was holding them, Pharoah of Egypt, was stronger than they were.

So they cried out to God, knowing their covenantal rights previously given to their ancestors Abraham, Isaac, and Jacob. And God responded.

That's why one of the most powerful things we can do as Christians is to take Communion. When *you* find yourself in the midst of a bondage situation that you are unable to get out of, go before the Lord during Communion. When understood and carried out rightly, Communion is more powerful than any Twelve-Step program, counseling session, sermon, or book. Those things have their places, and they are helpful. But the most powerful thing that you can do to get out of a bondage situation is to go before God at the time of Communion and cry out to Him based on His covenantal agreement made to you.

That's why where I pastor at our church, we hold Communion every week. We have a designated time for Communion each Sunday, where everyone can come before the Lord and relate to Him from a covenantal perspective. The rest of the service you are either listening to the choir or to the preacher; maybe you sing several songs in worship and join in corporate prayer. But the purpose of coming to church includes making a covenantal connection with the one, true God.

That's what makes prayer powerful. That's what makes Communion powerful. What makes them powerful is the legal arrangement that you have through the sacrifice of Jesus Christ and your relationship with the Holy Spirit.

When you understand the authority that comes from the new covenant, it changes everything. It is the key to your power to get heaven to manifest itself on earth. It is the power to bring His presence into your circumstances.

But don't just believe me because I preached it somewhere or wrote it in this book. I challenge you to try it yourself. Go out there and apply this truth to your life. See what God will do.

Whatever it is that you are in bondage to, or whatever is holding you in a trick bag, take what God says about that situation and present it to God. Present His Word back to Him. Find everything in the Bible that He has said on the matter, including His promises to you, and tell it all back to Him. Then watch what God can do in the middle of your trick bag.

You will be able to say, "Relationship, you are no longer going to define my existence. Circumstances, you are no longer going to dictate my moods. Job, you are no longer going to deflate my enthusiasm. Poor health, you are no longer going to keep me captive. Alcohol, you are no longer going to control my mind. Money, you are no longer going to dominate my choices. Pornography, you are no longer going to demean my joy." Whatever it is, you will be able to cry out to God in line with the covenant of His Word that He has given.

He will hear you in your trick bag just like He heard Israel. He will respond when you call out to Him according to His Word. Don't give up. Claim your rights before heaven in line with the new covenant of Jesus Christ.

You will see, as we will uncover in the next chapter, how the Israelites saw that God is a God who remembers His covenant.

IN THE HARD PLACES

1. Pastor Evans is first annoyed, then irritated, and finally frustrated by Bob #2. But Bob #2 becomes God's surprise blessing who delivers Pastor Evans' church from between a rock and a hard place. Were you surprised like Pastor Evans? Why does God sometimes do things in ways we would never expect?

2. When you are handed a trick-bag situation, "don't give up. Hang in there. Keep on pushing through," Pastor Evans says. Why should we hang in there and not despair?

3. Though the future nation of Israel grew in Egypt, its people remained enslaved by the Egyptians for more than four hundred years (Exodus 12:40–41). Then they sighed and cried out for God to deliver them. Why did He deliver them, according to Exodus 2:24?

4. While the Abrahamic, Mosaic, Davidic, and Palestinian covenants are all legally based, the new covenant is both spiritually and legally based. What three actions of Jesus (listed in "Our Covenantal Rights") entitle believers in Christ to partake of the blessing of the new covenant?

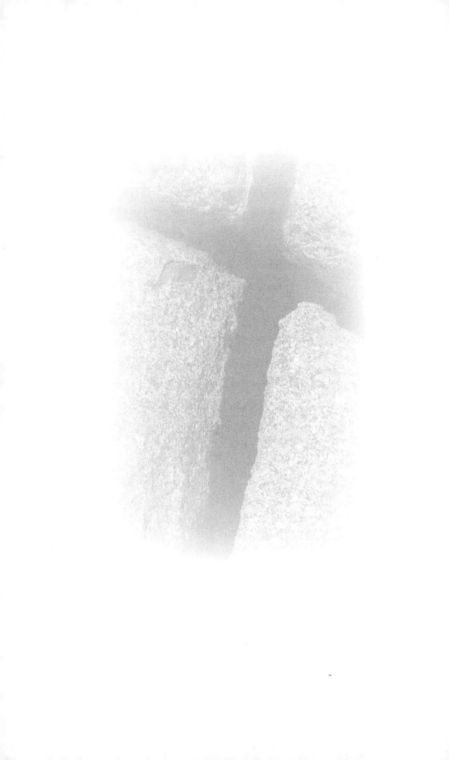

4

Moses and the Israelites

WAIT FOR GOD'S TIME

SHEEP MUST BE the dumbest animals God ever created. A sheep farmer once told me that sheep are so dumb that one of them will start walking in circles and the others will follow it, thinking that it is going somewhere.

That's why I can't imagine a job that could be any more frustrating than that of herding sheep. But that's exactly where we find our main character in the story of the Israelites when we pick back up in Exodus.

We read, "Now Moses was pasturing the flock of Jethro his father-in-law, priest of Midian; and he led the flock to the west side of the wilderness and came to Horeb, the mountain of God" (Exodus 3:1).

Before we move on, let's do a quick review of Moses. Supernaturally delivered from certain death as a baby when his mother hid him in a basket on the Nile River, Moses was discovered by Pharaoh's daughter and raised like royalty in Pharaoh's house. Moses had an inkling of his purpose as an adult, believing that he was to deliver his people from bondage.

Stephen summarizes Moses' background in Acts 7:

> Pharaoh's daughter took him away and nurtured him as her own son. Moses was educated in all the learning of the Egyptians, and he was a man of power in words and deeds. But when he was approaching the age of forty, it entered his mind to visit his brethren, the sons of Israel. And when he saw one of them being treated unjustly, he defended him and took vengeance for the oppressed by striking down the Egyptian. And he supposed that his brethren understood that God was granting them deliverance through him, but they did not understand. On the following day he appeared to them as they were fighting together, and he tried to reconcile them in peace, saying, "Men, you are brethren, why do you injure one another?" But the one who was injuring his neighbor pushed him away, saying "Who made you a ruler and judge over us? You do not mean to kill me as you killed the Egyptian yesterday, do you?" At this remark, Moses fled and became an alien in the land of Midian, where he became the father of two sons. (vv. 21–29)

A GREAT GOD, THE WRONG TIME

Moses believed that his purpose was to deliver his people, thinking "that his brethren understood that God was granting them deliverance through him." Because Moses believed this, his actions reflected it. But as is the case with many of us, Moses had a sense of destiny without the proper sense of timing. He tried to force something that God had not yet unveiled. He tried to make something happen when it wasn't the right time. He used human effort, logic, and strategy to attempt to accomplish a divine goal.

The goal was great: Deliver God's people. His strategy and timing, however, were off. And because they were off, Moses ended up moving from the White House to the outhouse. He spent the next forty years of his life in exile on the backside of a desert; there he herded dumb sheep.

Those forty years weren't wasted, though, as Exodus soon reveals. Because Moses would one day be called upon to lead the lost sheep of the house of Israel, God gave him experience leading sheep through a wilderness. God's delays are often tied to our development.

TIME TO DEVELOP MATURITY

Not only that, but God's delays are also tied to His creating, or allowing, a scenario that will be most ideal for His purpose. While God was developing Moses, He was also making a spiritual link between the condition of the Israelites and Moses' own maturity. Moses thought he was ready to deliver Israel. He had the education, wealth, eloquence, power, and raw materials to do it. But he didn't have a dependence on God shown in spiritual maturity, or humility. God is always after developing our spiritual maturity before bringing us into our destiny.

He does the same thing with the Israelites, as we will see later in the passage. He tells them that He is going to deliver them from Egypt and take them to the Promised Land, but what He doesn't tell them is that they will get there by way of a wilderness. To go from deliverance to destiny, they must first pass through development. The early verses in Deuteronomy 8 reveal this: "You shall remember all the way which the Lord your God has led you in the wilderness these forty years, that He might humble you. . . . He humbled you and let you be hungry, and fed you with manna which you did not know, nor did your fathers know, that He might make you understand that man does not live by bread alone, but man lives by everything that proceeds out of the mouth of the Lord" (vv. 2–3). The process was first deliverance, then development, and finally destiny.

Scripture tells us "without faith it is impossible to please [God]" (Hebrews 11:6). Like muscles, faith has to be developed. Moses didn't know what God was doing by having him stuck in yet another culture in the middle of a wilderness for forty long years. The Israelites didn't know what God was doing to solve their problem as they cried out to him. They definitely weren't daydreaming about a shepherd from Midian. But God was getting ready to make a divine intersection where He was arranging both situations to meet at the proper time.

These divine intersections are God-ordained points of connection that only He knows beforehand. Like the ram being led up the other side of the mountain as Abraham and Isaac hiked up to the altar, God knew that they would meet even though Abraham did not. That's why we can't force things to happen with God. We can't force our destiny. We don't know what God has coming up the other side of the mountains in our lives. We don't know what, where, or how God is going to arrange His divine intersection. All we can do is proceed with our development, trusting God to bring us to the point where we are ready for that connection at the proper time.

That's what Moses did. He did his job. He tended his sheep. But notice exactly where Moses tended his sheep. He was at "Horeb, the mountain of God" (Exodus 3:1). Moses was in the presence of God. He was doing his everyday task, that of leading sheep, purposefully in the presence of God. The thing that we can learn from this verse is that the place for you and me to go when we're in a time of personal development in a wilderness is into His presence. That's more than a sermon, a seminar, or a song. That is being desperate for Him. That is saying, "Even though I don't see anything or feel anything right now from You, God, I am still going to hang out in Your presence because I know that if I do, I will find You."

IN GOD'S PRESENCE:
A BUSH AFIRE

Moses is hanging out in God's presence when all of a sudden, he sees a bush afire. We read:

> The angel of the Lord appeared to him in a blazing fire from the midst of a bush; and he looked, and behold, the bush was burning with fire, yet the bush was not consumed. So Moses said, "I must turn aside now and see this marvelous sight, why the bush is not burned up." When the Lord saw that he turned aside to look, God called to him from the midst of the bush and said, "Moses, Moses!" And he said, "Here I am." (vv. 2–4)

We're told from this passage that the Angel of the Lord, the preincarnate Christ, is in the midst of the bush that is on fire. But Moses didn't know that. All Moses knew was that there was a bush on fire and yet it was not burned up. Before we move on, I want to tell you a secret that comes out of this scenario, how you can recognize when God is showing up in your rock-and-a-hard-place situation.

Theologians call what happened in this burning bush the shekinah glory, the visible manifestation of God. By His nature, God is invisible; He is spirit. But when God wants to make Himself visible, He can display His glory in a way that you can know it is He showing up.

How do you know when it is God showing up? In this situation, we know because we have a bush that is on fire and yet it is not consumed. In other words, a bush on fire is nothing special in a hot wilderness. If you are in a hot wilderness, stuff gets dry, and a fire starts. There's nothing unique about a fire in a bush in the wilderness. But a blazing bush that is not consumed by the fire? That's not normal. That's not expected. That's when you know it is God.

SOMETHING EXTRAORDINARY

How do you know when God is ready to break through your rock-and-a-hard-place situation? He will invade your ordinary with something extraordinary. He will create a scenario that doesn't make sense.

When God creates a scenario that doesn't make sense, it is not supposed to make sense. Don't ignore God showing up in a way that you can't explain. The reason you can't explain it is because it is God showing up in it. The Bible is replete with examples of a person or a group of people wedged between a rock and a hard place who saw God show up in a way that their human understanding couldn't explain.

If you are between a rock and a hard place and can't find a good way out of what seems like a never-ending situation, look for God to show up in a way that you can't explain. His ways are not your ways. His thoughts are not your thoughts (read Isaiah 55:8–9). God is not like you or me. If God were living in the era of soul music, His favorite song would be, "Didn't I (Blow Your Mind This Time)?"[1] Didn't I show up in a way that you couldn't explain? That's what God does. Look for it.

Moses saw the bush that wasn't burned up and probably thought, *I don't understand. I've been out here for forty years, and I've never seen anything like this. I must turn aside, because I can't ignore what I can't explain.* So he turned aside.

Please note from Exodus 3:4 that God did not reveal Himself to Moses until Moses turned aside to look. In other words, Moses had to act before God acted. Remember what we learned from the life of Abraham? Much of what God wants to do with us will take place when we move. Your movement will incite His movement. In our last chapter, we read, "When Israel cried to the Lord, He remembered His covenant." And in our current passage, we see, "When the Lord saw that he turned aside to look, God called . . ."

Until Moses responded to what God had placed before him, God wouldn't give him more. A lot of us want more from God, but we haven't turned to look at what He's already doing. We haven't responded to what He's already done. We don't do anything, and then we wonder why we aren't getting more.

We aren't getting more because God doesn't see us doing anything with what He's just given us. He just gave Moses something that he had never seen before—a bush that would not burn. He couldn't ignore that. When something cannot be explained in our lives, we need to turn aside and take a look at it as well because it could be God trying to show us something at another level.

WHEN GOD CALLS OUR NAME

When Moses turned aside, he heard two words, "Moses, Moses." It had probably been forty years since he had heard those words from God, "Moses, Moses." That is significant. When you've been trapped in a wilderness and life is going nowhere because of a wrong decision you made forty years earlier, you don't want a sermon addressed to the general congregation. You want God calling your name, "Moses, Moses."

God often deals with us collectively as a church body, but He also deals with us individually. When your pastor teaches the Word of God, there is truth that applies to the corporate group of believers. Theologians call this *Logos*, the Word of God. But when you are stranded in a wilderness or between a rock and a hard place, you also need a word *from* God. This is called *rhema*, when you hear a word from God for you. Rhema is for those times when you need a direct word from God with your name on it.

The job of the Holy Spirit in the new covenant is to allow God to call your name. That is why you are indwelled with the Holy Spirit. The function of the Holy Spirit is to personalize the word from God to you while still being true to the written Word of God. That doesn't mean He changes the written Word of God. The Bible is complete and finished with Revelation. The book of Revelation literally means "The End." However, even though the Bible is complete in its revelation, its application goes on individually and specifically.

This is a problem that often shows up in fundamentalism. Fundamentalism exegetes the Word of God so that a person can understand it without necessarily applying it. Fundamentalists often want you to understand the text by reading books, commentaries and concordances. But you can be a great biblical scholar and never hear God's voice calling your name.

"ABRAHAM" . . . "MOSES" . . . "TONY"

In our first two chapters, we saw that God called, "Abraham, Abraham." Now, we see God calling, "Moses, Moses." What you should want to hear more than anything else as long as you live is God calling out your name. That's rhema, a word from God.

I'll never forget the time when God called, "Tony, Tony." Lois and I had been married a few years and we had young children. We were struggling financially because I was working full time while going to school full time to get my master's degree from Dallas Theological Seminary (DTS). We did what we could to make our ends meet, but things were tight.

I was getting ready to finish my master's degree and begin the long process of working on my doctorate at DTS. A number of options became available on how to do that. One of the more promising was to serve on the faculty of the seminary. DTS had extended an invitation to me to work full time as a professor while getting my doctorate. A couple of other ministry opportunities also presented themselves at this time.

Then, there was this crazy idea of starting a church in our home with just ten people. No consistent salary. No job security. None of that. It was just an idea to start a church with pretty much my own family and a few others.

I knew which way logic would take me, but I didn't know which way to go. I came up with different rationales for different options, but I didn't know which option God would have me choose. I didn't want to flip a coin, not on a decision as big as this. I also didn't want to choose one and hope that God would bless it. Instead, Lois and I made a commitment together to pray to God that He would bring clarity to our situation. We prayed that He would show up in a way that we would know that it was Him providing the direction.

During that time, we were invited over to dinner with some other couples to the home of Charles Ryrie, a professor of mine at the seminary (and editor of the Ryrie Study Bible). So there we were sitting and talking at the home of Dr. Ryrie, when he said something—to this day I cannot remember his exact words. But when he made the statement, it was as if time stood still. I looked at Lois. Lois looked at me. We looked at each other immediately because as soon as the words came out of his mouth, we knew that we had the clarity we had been asking God for.

The Holy Spirit tattooed our names on Dr. Ryrie's statement, making it reach beyond our audible ears and into our inner man and woman. The Holy Spirit speaks deep into our being. At that moment, the Holy Spirit told both Lois and I to start the church in our home, and our direction was confirmed by our unity on it.

God is still in the business of calling our names. What we need to do is do like Moses, and say, "Here I am." Then do what He says.

DIRT WITH GOD ON IT

Moses says, "Here I am." He's on his way to take a closer look at this marvelous sight when God stops him. We read, "Do not come near here; remove your sandals from your feet, for the place on which you are standing is holy ground" (Exodus 3:5). First, God calls Moses by name, and then He stops Moses in his tracks.

Let's look at this before moving on. To take off your shoes is to identify with your place because, on your best day, you are nothing more than dignified dirt. It's important for us to understand this. We came from the ground. When we die, we're going back to the ground.

In fact, everyone reading this book is worth not much more than $3.57. It's true. When you boil down all of the components that make you up and connect them with their value in the ground, you are worth around $3.57. I'm not trying to be harsh, but that's why you or I can't think too highly of ourselves. We're worth $3.57. When you get home to your house in the suburbs, it's $3.57 living in the suburbs. It's $3.57 wearing designer clothes. It's $3.57 with more money in the bank than you are actually worth.

God said, "Moses, take off your shoes. I need to remind you who you really are—not much more than dignified dirt."

But now it's not just dirt because God tells Moses he is standing on holy ground. It's dirt with God on it. It's now dirt with God wanting to do something through it. It's set apart.

Before God can intervene in our rock-and-a-hard-place situations and use us, He must humble you and me. He must remind us of who we are. Take off your shoes. Humble yourself. Go low in the presence of holiness. Because anything higher than dirt is too high if you want to be used by God. Anything above the ground— whether you wear quarter-inch leather soles or quarter-inch heels—is too high.

Moses' removal of his sandals signified his position as a creature underneath the Creator. It said, "God, I called the shots forty years ago in Egypt. I've been calling the shots with these sheep. But You call the shots now because I recognize You as Creator over me."

A DIVINE INTERSECTION

Moses took off his sandals. And then God said,

"I am the God of your father, the God of Abraham, the God of Isaac, and the God of Jacob." Then Moses hid his face, for he was afraid to look at God. The Lord said, "I have surely seen the affliction of My people who are in Egypt, and have given heed to their cry because of their taskmasters, for I am aware of their sufferings. So I have come down to deliver them from the power of the Egyptians, and to bring them up from that land to a good and spacious land, to a land flowing with milk and honey . . . Therefore, come now, and I will send you to Pharaoh, so that you may bring My people, the sons of Israel, out of Egypt." (3:6–10)

This is where we see God making His divine intersection. He says that He is going to deliver a whole nation of people from a whole nation of oppressors and that He's going to use Moses to do it. Now wait a minute—didn't Moses know that he was supposed to do that forty years ago? He did, but remember, this is an issue of timing. God may tell you many things over a long period of time, but He will always wait until everyone is ready. The circumstances had to be just right for all of the groups of people in order for Him to make His divine connection.

Forty years later and the scenario is ripe for the intersection—although now Moses has become a little more than humble. He actually has become too humble and tells God that he can't do it (v. 11). The Tony Evans' translation of God's response is, "Moses, hush your fuss. Go!"

So Moses went. We read in Exodus 5, "And afterward Moses and Aaron came and said to Pharaoh, 'Thus says the Lord, the God of Israel, "Let My people go that they may celebrate a feast to Me in the wilderness"'" (v. 1).

CAUGHT BETWEEN A VERY BIG ROCK
AND A VERY HARD PLACE

So now we are at Israel's very big rock and very hard place, probably the most celebrated event in Israel's history. God, through Moses, has brought ten plagues against Egypt. Finally Pharaoh relents, and God is ready to lead Israel out of captivity. The exodus begins. But the rock and hard place are not far away. If we flip a few pages over to Exodus 14, we learn how it developed:

> The Lord hardened the heart of Pharaoh, king of Egypt, and he chased after the sons of Israel as the sons of Israel were going out boldly. . . . Then they said to Moses, "Is it because there were no graves in Egypt that you have taken us away to die in the wilderness? Why have you dealt with us in this way, bringing us out of Egypt? Is this not the word that we spoke to you in Egypt, saying 'Leave us alone that we may serve the Egyptians'? For it would have been better for us to serve the Egyptians than to die in the wilderness." (vv. 8–12)

Isn't that what we do when we get caught between a rock and a hard place? We act just like the Israelites, fussing and complaining.

Moses replies to their complaints by telling them to stand still and to be quiet, which is similar to how God had replied to him when he came across the burning bush. Moses said, "'Do not fear! Stand by and see the salvation of the Lord which He will accomplish for you today; for the Egyptians whom you have seen today, you will never see them again forever. The Lord will fight for you while you keep silent'" (vv.13–14).

Moses acknowledges to the Israelites that they are stuck. There is Egypt on one side and the Red Sea on the other. They are trapped. But he tells them not to worry and to stand by to see what God will do.

I have a feeling that it wasn't too hard for the Israelites to agree to stand by, since going back meant the Egyptians were going to kill them, and going forward meant they were going to drown in the Red Sea. The Israelites were literally caught between a rock and a hard place. There was no way to turn. There were no options to choose. The only advice they got from their leader was to be still and keep their mouths shut.

Verse 15 reveals that all the while Moses was telling the Israelites to stand by and see the deliverance of the Lord, he was crying out to God. On one hand, he's saying, "Hey, don't sweat it. God's got it." Then on the other hand, he's crying out to God, "We're stuck! God, do something!"

Have you ever done a similar thing in your rock-and-a-hard-place situation? You're telling the people around you, "It's going to be okay," while at the same time turning to God and saying when no one else is looking, "Are you out of your mind, God? There is no way out of this!" If you have done that, then you're in good company because Moses was doing the same exact thing:

> Then the Lord said to Moses, "Why are you crying out to Me? Tell the sons of Israel to go forward. As for you, lift up your staff and stretch out your hand over the sea and divide it, and the sons of Israel shall go through the midst of the sea on dry land. As for Me, behold, I will harden the hearts of the Egyptians so that they will go in after them; and I will be honored through Pharaoh and all his army, through his chariots and his horsemen." (vv. 15–17)

God says two essential things in His talk to Moses. First, He says, "As for you, Moses, do this." And then He says, "As for Me, I will do this." He says, "Moses, first you need to act. You need to take that little stick that you've been using to lead sheep around, and you need to hold that out, because it is now sanctified."

HOLDING A STICK AND WATCHING GOD ACT

In other words, God says that He's not going to do His role until Moses first does his. He wants Moses to step out in faith. Not only that, but He asks Moses to step out in faith with the very object He spent forty years of development with in the wilderness. He wants Moses to use the staff that he led his sheep with for all of those years.

A lot of what God wants to do in your life and in mine is similar to this situation. He will not move until we first move according to what He has revealed to us. A lot of what He asks us to do is often tied to the very things we learned, used, and developed during our wilderness times.

Our move isn't always all that huge. Just like Moses' move wasn't all that huge. All God was asking him to do was to hold out his stick. If Moses would just hold out his stick, then God said that He'd do all of the big stuff. He'd open the Red Sea, harden Pharaoh's heart, make him go in after them, and close the Red Sea.

To reveal the faith within us, God often asks us to do our little thing first. Hold out our sticks. Take that step. Make the move. Quit the job to stay at home. Accept the job that He has shown. Stop the habit. Curb the tongue. Go to church. Go overseas. Whatever it is that He is revealing to you, God will often wait to do His big thing until you do what He has asked you to do.

He does this because He wants us to see Him in a way we've never seen Him before. He wants us to experience Him in a way that we've never seen Him before. He wants us to see the connection between our act of faith and His deliverance. He wants to be more than just a cosmic Santa Claus with a pocketful of miracles to throw down. God wants a relationship with each of us. He wants you to see Him up close and personal. So He puts you in a situation where He is your only solution. Where it can't be fixed if He doesn't fix it. He says, "I've let you use all of the natural options available to you, and you are still stuck. Well then, you are stuck with a purpose. Now, what I want you to do is to go to the mountain of God and enter My presence and see what supernatural thing I do to call your name personally so that you can experience Me at a whole new level."

But before He does anything at all, He often asks us to hold out our sticks.

You might feel silly holding out a small stick over a huge body of water that doesn't seem to be going anywhere. But if you'll do it when He asks you to do it, He'll do everything that He has promised as well. Just like He did for the Israelites when He led them through a sea on dry land.

WHAT GOD DOES
FOR YOU, IN YOU, AND THROUGH YOU

When the Israelites got to the other side of the Red Sea and they saw how God had closed the waters on top of the Egyptian horses and their riders, they broke into song (Exodus 15). Their complaints changed to a chorus because now they had seen God firsthand. Now, they had a testimony.

When God takes you from your rock-and-a-hard-place situation, you will have a testimony. God won't be God anymore because of what He did in somebody else's life. God won't be God because of what some preacher told you about Him.

Now, God will be God to you because God has been God for you.

He has been God in you.

He has been God through you.

He has intervened in your human circumstances in a way that is only explainable and explicable by Him.

That's what you want. You don't always want to be living your life with a prayer request. You want to be living your life with a testimony of what God can do because of what God has done for you, in you, and through you.

NOTE

1. "Didn't I (Blow Your Mind This Time)?" is a popular song by The Delfonics released in 1970. It won a Grammy Award for the best R&B performance by a duo or group.

IN THE HARD PLACES

1. Hebrews 11:6 reveals that to please God we must have faith. And faith, "like muscles," has to be developed over time. How did God develop faith in Moses—and in the Israelites?

2. "God is not like you or me." Sometimes He shows His presence in a powerful way, whether through a visible manifestation (the bush that burned without being consumed that Moses beheld) or through invading our ordinary life with something extraordinary. Can you recall a time when you or someone you know watched God show that His "ways [are] higher than your ways" (Isaiah 55:9)? What did you learn about God?

3. God delivered Moses and the Israelites from Pharaoh's mighty hand and cruel slavery after ten miraculous plagues. But after that deliverance he put the people's backs against the wall at the Red Sea. It made no sense! What does this tell you about God's plans and power?

4. After the Israelites had crossed the Red Sea and then watched the waters collapse upon the Egyptian army, what did the people do? Why?

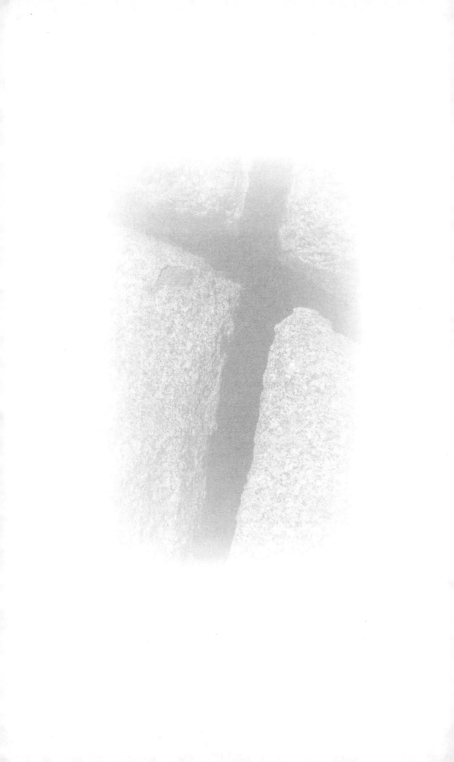

5

COME CLOSE TO GOD DURING THE WILD RIDE

WHEN LOIS AND I started dating, I came up with a strategy to encourage her to fall more in love with me. She was a lot in love with me from the beginning, but I wanted to increase that.

What I decided to do was to take her to the amusement park. Once we had wandered around the amusement park for a while and had enjoyed some of the games and food, I coolly asked her if she wanted to ride the Wild Mouse. Lois had never been on the Wild Mouse ride before, but I had. I knew how *wild* the Wild Mouse really was. She didn't have any idea because it looked like an innocent ride.

Back in the 1960s, the Wild Mouse was a wooden roller coaster with cars so small that they could only fit two adults side by side. (Some of those coaster cars are still around today at certain amusement parks.) The mouse coasters had been designed to take tight turns and short bunny hops, producing high lateral G-forces. The Wild Mouse gave the impression that you were going to fly right off of the edge of the track before it turned.

I knew Lois's personality and that going on the Wild Mouse would be a tough situation for her. But I hadn't told her that. I had only mentioned that we should go on a nice ride together.

So we got on the Wild Mouse. The car began to shoot out at key turns, making it seem like our small vehicle would fly right off of the edge of the track. Lois screamed. Then she scooted closer to me. Our car veered to the right and then shot out again, making it feel like we were going to zoom straight out into midair. Lois screamed again. Then she scooted even closer to me this time. By the end of the ride, Lois wasn't sitting far away from me at all. She was sitting as close as possible. That had been my plan.

I had wanted Lois to sit closer all along. The Wild Mouse accomplished that.

Sometimes God puts us on a wild ride. We find ourselves strapped in, cramped between a rock and a hard place. Life seems to be out of our control. God allows these situations for many reasons, as we have already seen through the lives of Abraham, Moses, and the Israelites, but one of them is because trials can bring us closer to Him. I didn't say that trials automatically bring us closer to Him—a lot of that has to do with how we respond. But trials *can* bring us closer to Him.

A CLOSER, BIGGER VIEW OF GOD

When we get closer to God, we experience His presence, power, and protection. Our faith grows, and in that growth we discover an uncommon peace. We also get a bigger view of God in the process —a super-sized view.

Getting a bigger view of God is like having a bigger portion at McDonald's. When I pull up to McDonald's and order a meal, the voice on the other side of the speaker asks me, "Do you want to super-size that?" By asking me if I want to super-size my order, she's letting me know that for just a little bit more, I can get larger fries, a larger sandwich, and a larger drink. For just a little bit more on my part, I can get a lot more from McDonald's.

Trick-bag trials are those situations when God asks us to go just a little bit more than we've ever gone before in our faith. He tells us that if we will trust Him a little bit more, step out a little bit more, let go a little bit more . . . then we will experience God like we've never known Him before. These kinds of trials are designed to super-size God in our lives. They give us a relationship with Him that is not only closer and more intimate, but that is bigger than the norm.

OBEDIENCE THAT LEADS TO A STORM

That's what happened to the disciples of Jesus following a busy day of ministry. We read in Mark 6, "Immediately Jesus made His disciples get into the boat and go ahead of Him to the other side to Bethsaida, while He Himself was sending the crowd away. After bidding them farewell, He left for the mountain to pray. When it was evening, the boat was in the middle of the sea, and He was alone on the land" (vv. 45–47).

Here is one of a number of scenarios in Scripture where Jesus develops His disciples in an arena where they are already familiar. Many of the disciples came from a fishing background. Not only did they live around the Sea of Galilee, but they spent a large amount of time in boats on it. As the lowest freshwater lake on earth at seven hundred feet below sea level, the Sea of Galilee is a large lake, stretching thirteen miles across at its widest point. At Bethsaida, where the disciples boarded, the lake is eight miles across. The location of the sea in the Jordan Rift causes tempests to flare up violently with little or no notice.

Having spent so much time on the water, the disciples no doubt had experienced these storms before. But what they went through on this night tested more than their boating expertise; it tested their hope.

Jesus had just completed performing one of the greatest miracles of all, the feeding of the five thousand. We will take a closer look at this miracle in the next chapter. After He fed the five thousand and dismissed them, Jesus told His disciples to get into the boat ahead of Him and go to the other side.

The disciples did exactly what Jesus had told them to do. They got into the boat, at night, and took out across the sea. The disciples got into the boat just like Jesus had said, in obedience. Make sure that you remember that it was in their obedience that the disciples ran directly into a storm.

Then the winds came and the waves whipped up the lake. As Mark reports,

> Seeing them straining at the oars, for the wind was against them, at about the fourth watch of the night [Jesus] came to them, walking on the sea; and He intended to pass by them. But when they saw Him walking on the sea, they supposed that it was a ghost, and cried out; for they all saw Him and were terrified. But immediately He spoke with them and said to them, 'Take courage; it is I, do not be afraid.' Then He got into the boat with them,

and the wind stopped; and they were utterly astonished, for they had not gained any insight from the incident of the loaves, but their heart was hardened. (6:48–52)

The disciples' obedience literally took them into the nucleus of a disaster.

I want you to remember that because it is a helpful illustration for our own lives. I wish I could tell you that following Jesus means that the waters of life will always be calm. I wish I could tell you that following Jesus means life will be rosy and all of your days sweet. But I can't. These disciples were following Jesus, and they ran right into rough seas. The disciples discovered, as many of us have also discovered, that you can be both in the center of God's will and still in a storm.

There is a lot of preaching today and many Christian books that tell you that if you follow Jesus you will never have to face any challenges in life. That wasn't true for Jesus, or for anyone else I know who has followed Him. In fact, some of us didn't have any troubles at all until we started following Jesus.

Following Jesus doesn't give you immunity from troubles. What it does give you is the opportunity to experience Him in the midst of the trouble, as we will see later. Life comes with troubles, regardless of whether or not you follow Jesus. You get to choose if you want Him to join you in your troubles or if you'd rather go through them alone.

Remember, in the boat the disciples were in the center of God's will. Jesus had led them directly into a storm, which brings us to our first set of contradictions. For starters, verse 48 says that they were, "straining at the oars, for the wind was against them." The King James Version says, "The wind was contrary unto them." As they rowed in one direction, the wind roared in the other. They were doing exactly what Jesus had asked them to do, and in doing it they found resistance.

The wind fought against them. The rain tried to drown them. No doubt they questioned why Jesus had sent them across the lake at night.

TO QUESTION THE HEART OF GOD

That's a question many of us might raise when we find ourselves having been sent by God directly into a storm. We're not asking Jesus why He sent us out on a boat, but we are asking Him why we ended up between a rock and a hard place when our obedience to Him actually took us there to begin with. That's the most difficult kind of trick bag, because it makes us question the heart of God. After all, we had stepped out in faith, but when we did, the very act of doing it led us straight into the storm.

Not only were the disciples straining against the storm, but they were also struggling, as we have just read, "about the fourth watch of the night." That would be between 3 and 6 a.m. It was the dark just before the dawn. The disciples were not only in a contrary situation when they faced resistance, but they couldn't see clearly either. It was probably pitch-black all around them.

That's often the case with us, isn't it? When we are pressed between a rock and a hard place, God can appear like a blur. You don't hear Him. You don't see Him. It's dark. It's the final watch of the night. Nothing seems clear.

A number of emotions come out during those times: worry, doubt, fear. Another one is hopelessness. We all know what it feels like to experience hopelessness to varying degrees. In fact, many people define hopelessness as looking forward to something that they know they will never get, seeing no possibility for improvement or change. Many of us today are drowning in a sea of hopelessness surrounded by a land of emptiness where there seems to be no way out.

ROW FORWARD OR TURN BACK?

The question is this: Do you keep trying to get where God has told you to go even though it's difficult to keep going in that direction? Or do you do the easier thing, which means turning around and going back to where you had begun by using the wind behind you to push you there?

That's the dilemma that comes up in a trick bag. Do you turn around and use the wind to work with you, all the while being disobedient? Or do you do what Jesus had said and go forward in His will, even though it now seems not only risky, but also impossible? Obeying God can mean running into rough waters. It can plant you right in the middle of a contradiction, between a rock and a hard place. You're trying to do what God asked you to do, but He has sent the wind to assail you.

It's in those times when we are trying on the outside that hopelessness can creep into the inside. The disciples were trying. I'll give them that much. We read in the passage that Jesus, "seeing them straining at the oars," had decided to come to them. If they were "straining at the oars," then they were trying. They were out there grunting, groaning, and using everything within them to fight this storm. Struggling as hard as they could to do exactly what Jesus had told them to do, yet they were still stuck.

JESUS PRAYS AND WATCHES

Meanwhile, Jesus is praying (v. 46). As the disciples are straining against the wind, Jesus is praying. Get this—Jesus is off somewhere, praying! Jesus can be praying at the wrong times sometimes, it seems. When life is caving in all around those who are following Him, He's headed off to a prayer meeting.

Don't read the Scripture passage too quickly. If we look closer, we realize it's not a typical prayer meeting, full of general praises and routine requests. Jesus had gone there to pray in light of what He knew He was getting ready to put His disciples through. How do I know that He was praying about what they were going through? Because verse 48 tells us. He saw them "straining at the oars."

Jesus is praying on a mountain, but He is still in the middle of their mess. He's praying, while at the same time watching. This is a very interesting situation because not only is it the fourth watch of the night—total darkness—but they are also four miles out in the middle of the sea. I'm not sure how anyone can see anybody straining at anything in the middle of the night, and over four miles away. That is, unless you are both God and man completely.

What happens at this prayer meeting is that Jesus parlays His divinity while identifying with their humanity. Only Christ can do both because, as we saw earlier as we looked at the life of Abraham, Jesus is our High Priest who also sympathizes with our humanity (see Hebrews 4:15). That's what makes Jesus the best prayer warrior ever. Not only does He see us from a divine viewpoint, but He also identifies with our struggles.

It is one thing to understand intellectually what someone else is experiencing. It is another thing to know it firsthand. For example, a male obstetrician can understand from an informational standpoint what a pregnant woman in labor is going through because he has read the books, and he has participated in a number of deliveries. But a female obstetrician who has also had a baby herself can empathize with the woman in delivery. She not only has the information; she also has the experience.

When Jesus sees us between a rock and a hard place, He not only understands what we are going through from an informational standpoint, but He also knows what it is like to have gone through something where there seems to be no good way out. He has cried out to His Father before, "My God, My God, why have you forsaken me?" (Matthew 27:46).

No doubt the disciples felt forsaken as they strained against the fierce winds. Jesus' prayer for them, just like His prayer for us when we are in a trick bag, could have resembled His prayer for Peter that Peter's faith would not fail (Luke 22:32). He prayed that in spite of what Peter was about to go through, his circumstances would not overrule his faith.

When we find ourselves caught between a rock and a hard place, we too tend to question God. Our tendency to lose faith is like Israel's when they were taken out of Egypt and thought that they had been left in the wilderness to die either by the Egyptians chasing them or by drowning in the Red Sea. It is easy to question God and lose sight of His goodness because of the negatives that have come about.

OPEN YOUR EYES WIDE

But when you feel like all is lost, *that* is the time to open your eyes the widest. You never know what you might see on a dark night. As we discovered when we read through the passage earlier, Jesus came to the disciples walking on the waves at night.

Jesus' solution is both strange and intriguing. Jesus came into their chaos by walking on the water. He entered their struggle while walking on the sea. I don't want you to miss this point, because Jesus walking *on* the water *is* the point.

Jesus is walking on top of their problem.

Their problem was the water. Jesus walked right on it. Water whipped by the wind had created havoc in their environment. Yet Jesus Christ came to them on top of the very thing that was causing them so much fear.

When we are in a trick bag, we generally look for God to take us out of our situation. That is a normal response because we don't want to be in conflict, confusion, or pain. But what God often wants to do is to join us *in* the trick bag.

A VERY HOT TRICK BAG

Isn't that what happened to my three boys—Shadrach, Meshach, and Abednego?

In Daniel 3, we read how King Nebuchadnezzar (I'll call him Nebbie for short), made a "decree that every man who hears the sound of the horn, flute, lyre, trigon, psaltery, and bagpipe and all kinds of music, is to fall down and worship the golden image. But whoever does not fall down and worship shall be cast into the midst of a furnace of blazing fire" (vv. 10–11).

Shadrach, Meshach, and Abednego obeyed God. They didn't worship the idol. So they were thrown into the blazing fire. God could have stopped them from being thrown into the fire. He could have put out the fire. He could have delivered them in a number of ways before they ever got into the fire. But He didn't. So Shadrach, Meshach, and Abednego, out of obedience to God, got tossed into a trick bag.

In they went. But, get this, so did God.

When Nebbie looked into the furnace, he said, "Was it not three men we cast bound into the midst of the fire?"

His officials replied, "Certainly, O King" (v. 24). What else could they say?

THE AMAZED KING

King Nebbie stood there dumbfounded. I can see him pointing his crooked finger and shouting, "Look! I see four men loosed and walking about in the midst of the fire without harm, and the appearance of the fourth is like a son of the gods!" (v. 25).

Nebbie is wondering, *Hey, didn't we tie these dudes up before we tossed them in? Why are they walking around free now—and who is that homeboy with them?*

Jesus had joined Shadrach, Meshach, and Abednego *in* their trick bag. By joining them *in* their trick bag, God not only got glory for Himself in the whole nation of Babylon, but He also gave the three boys a greater future than had been their past.

When the boys had been let out of the furnace, Nebuchadnezzar said, "I make a decree that any people, nation or tongue that speaks anything offensive against the God of Shadrach, Meshach and Abednego shall be torn limb from limb and their houses reduced to a rubbish heap, inasmuch as there is no other god who is able to deliver in this way" (v. 29). The King then caused Shadrach, Meshach, and Abednego to prosper in the province of Babylon. My three boys didn't just get delivered – they got their destiny!

They got their destiny because Jesus joined them in the middle of their trick bag. Just like He did with the disciples on the Sea of Galilee.

THE LOOKS ON THEIR FACES

I would have loved to have seen the looks on the disciples' faces when they saw Jesus walking toward them on the water. When I get to heaven, I'm going to ask for a rerun of this. I want to see the rerun of these twelve burly men in a small boat in the middle of a storm—screaming! The wind whips and howls all over the place. The boat rocks and tosses. Just standing up is nearly impossible. It's dark. It's wet. Someone's retching their dinner up over the side. It's dangerous. I can feel their fear. They are terrified that they are going to lose their lives.

Then, to make matters worse, they see what looks like a ghost come out of nowhere, walking on top of the water. If I had been there, I would have been screaming, too! It's bad enough that we're in a storm about to die, and now we have Casper's ugly brother here with us.

The disciples were so confused by the chaos that they didn't even recognize Jesus as He walked on the sea, and "they supposed that it was a ghost, and cried out" (Mark 6:49).

The disciples didn't expect a visitation like this. Seeing Jesus walk on the water toward them when they had left him hours earlier on dry land didn't seem like a real possibility. Jesus knew that they wouldn't be expecting Him to come to them on the water. He had been praying for them that their faith would not fail because He knew they would be disoriented in the storm. He knew they were straining to obey, straining to go exactly where God had told them to go—into a contradictory situation.

We know that Jesus had been praying for their faith not to fail because if we go back one verse earlier, we see a very interesting phrase. He "intended to pass by them." Hey, it's bad enough that you're coming in the dark, Jesus, and scaring me. But now you're saying that you are going to pass by me? Jesus had wanted to see their response before He made His decision to change from passing them by to joining them. Jesus had wanted to see if, in the middle of their trick bag, they would show any faith as He approached them.

"WHAT'S WRONG, GUYS?"

This isn't the only time when Jesus didn't reveal Himself early on, and instead waited for the response of those He had approached. Just after Jesus had been crucified, two disciples were walking on the road to Emmaus. The two men looked discouraged. Jesus came up to them, slightly camouflaged, and said, "What's wrong, guys?"

"They stood still, looking sad," Luke tells us. "One of them, named Cleopas, answered and said to Him, 'Are You the only one visiting Jerusalem and unaware of the things which have happened here in these days?'" (24:17–18). Cleopas went on and told Him more about what had happened.

Jesus replied, "'O foolish men and slow of heart to believe in all that the prophets have spoken!'". . . . Then beginning with Moses and with all the prophets, He explained to them the things concerning Himself in all the Scriptures" (vv. 25, 27). He talked to them about Himself, although they didn't know it was Jesus. He was doing a Bible study as they walked.

They finally got to their house, "and He acted as though He were going farther" (v. 28). The Bible study was over. He wasn't even going to stop. Jesus had planned to keep going. He was waiting to see what they were going to do with the information that they had just gotten from the Word. Because what they would do with it would determine whether He would stop and stay, or keep going.

The two men urged the stranger to stay with them. He agreed, went in, and broke the bread; and when He did, their eyes were opened. They recognized Him as the Son of God. As Jesus broke the bread, no doubt they saw the nail scars on His hands.

HOW TO MAKE IT PERSONAL:
FELLOWSHIP WITH GOD

Here is what had happened: When He walked with them, they got the Word *of* God, just as we looked at earlier in the life of Moses. The men on the road to Emmaus got the *logos*. But when they fellowshiped with Him in the house, they got a Word *from* God, *rhema*, because their eyes were opened. In other words, when He was just having a Bible study with them, they got spiritual truth. But spiritual knowledge alone did not open their eyes. Only when the Word of God led to fellowship with the Person of God did illumination set in so that they could see Jesus, the Christ.

The point is that Jesus had planned to walk by to see what they would do with the truth that they had received intellectually. He wanted to see whether it would lead to a personal relationship with Him, and personal interaction with Him, in order to give them illumination. Just having a formal Bible study wasn't going to cut it.

The question to them, and to the twelve main disciples, was: What are you going to do with what I told you? Are you going to keep it academic? Or is it going to be made personal? What are you going to do now that I've told you to go to the other side, disciples? Are you going to bail on me because you're now in a tempestuous trick bag? Or is your faith going to prevail in spite of your circumstances?

Jesus came by the boat to see how they would respond. They didn't recognize Him because they didn't expect Him. They didn't recognize Him because their eyes were focused on the water whipping around them. They didn't recognize Him because they strained to see anything in the darkness of the night.

The disciples missed Jesus at the moment that they needed Him the most.

I hate to say this, but I think that happens to many of us, too.

Thankfully, we have a Savior who not only calls out to us in the middle of the storm, but does some of His best work in the dark.

Let's see what that work is as we dig deeper into Mark 6 in the next chapter.

IN THE HARD PLACES

1. The disciples obeyed Jesus' command, and soon discovered "that you can be both in the center of God's will and still be in a storm." Does that truth—you can obey God's will and still encounter trouble— surprise you? Why or why not?

2. Pastor Evans reminds us of two other times Jesus appeared with followers who were in a hard place. In the first, three young men were tossed into a blazing furnace because they obeyed God. Jesus joined them in the form of the Angel of the Lord. What were the two outcomes after an amazed King Nebuchadnezzar saw this deliverance?

3. The second time Jesus appeared with His followers, on the road to Emmaus, the two men were devastated that Jesus, having died, apparently was not the Messiah they had hoped for (Luke 24:19–21). What happened because of His visit (vv. 31–35)?

4. Like the twelve disciples in the boat and the two disciples walking toward Emmaus, we may miss seeing Jesus when He is near us. Reread the final paragraphs of this chapter. Why do we sometimes miss seeing Jesus when He is ready to aid us during times we are between a rock and a hard place?

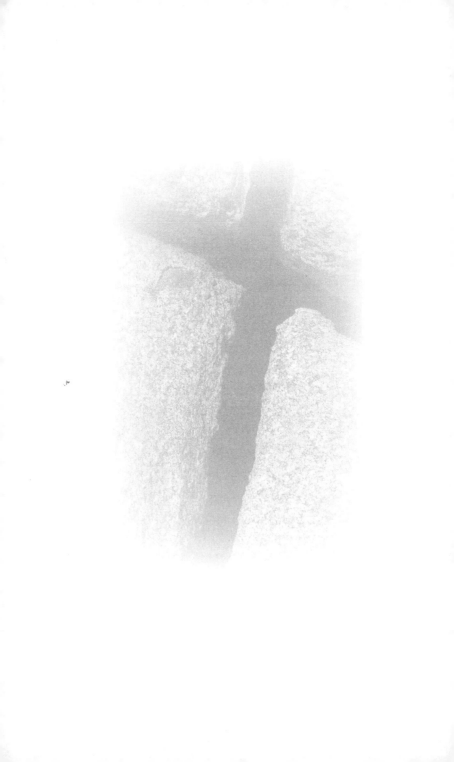

6

The Disciples

FIND CALM IN YOUR CHAOS

I LOVE THE GOSPELS. The beauty of the Gospels is that they often tell the same story from different angles. It's like viewing biblical truth through the lens of more than one camera. In biblical theology, Matthew, Mark, and Luke are known as the Synoptic Gospels because these three Gospels tell virtually all of the same stories.

It is helpful to compare notes from one Gospel to the next because by looking at all of them, we receive a more complete account of what happened. One Gospel writer might have left out something that another Gospel writer considered to be essential information.

In chapter 5, we left off with Jesus walking on the water toward the boat. The disciples think He is a ghost. The director yells cut.

We turn from Mark 6 to get Matthew's angle. Matthew gives us information that Mark doesn't include. Matthew zooms his lens in on Peter for the next scene.

THE STORM ON THE INSIDE

Before we focus on Peter, notice that Jesus identifies Himself to the terrified disciples. He says, "Take courage, it is I, do not be afraid" (Matthew 14:27). Obviously Jesus can see that these grown men are scared to death. He speaks to them to calm them on the inside before He ever addresses what is happening on the outside. The wind still roars. The waves still rage. The storm beats down all around them. But Jesus sees a different kind of storm inside of them, and addresses that first. He sees the internal storm, and calms them with His Word.

I'm sure many of you have been in a session with a Bible teacher or listening to a sermon on a Sunday when you were in the middle of turmoil. But just hearing the Word of God calmed you down significantly, even though it didn't change what you were facing.

That's precisely what happened here. The disciples heard the voice of Jesus and it spoke calm into their chaos. So much so that my boy Peter even relocated his courage and told Jesus, "Lord, if it is You, command me to come to You on the water" (v. 28).

Peter said, in essence, "Tell me to come, Jesus. I dare You."

ON TOP OF THE WATER

So Jesus bids Peter to come. Peter climbs over the edge of the boat and puts his feet where no finite man has ever been—on top of the water. Peter is now walking *on* the problem. The problem has not disappeared. In fact, the wind and the waves attack Peter even more now because he is out there in the midst of them. But because Peter is focused on Jesus Christ and Jesus has bid him to come, the problem no longer defines Peter's experience.

Until he lets it.

Matthew continues his account of the story by saying, "And Peter . . . walked on the water and came toward Jesus. But seeing the wind, he became frightened" (vv. 29–30). And then he began to sink.

INTO THE WATER

At first Peter is walking on the water. No problem. The storm doesn't seem nearly as bad as it did before Peter had heard Jesus' voice. But as Peter continues to walk on the water further, he begins to pay more attention to how bad his situation feels. He takes his eyes off Jesus and puts them on his circumstances. When he does, he begins to sink.

The fact that Peter begins to sink in this story is not the most interesting part to me. What's interesting to me is that Jesus lets him sink. Jesus sees Peter's eyes go off of Him and onto the storm. He doesn't yell out, "Pete, buddy—eyes back on Me! Right here, man! You're going down!"

No, He just lets him sink.

Why does Jesus let His children sink? Why does He let *us* sink when it seems like we've stepped out in faith and gotten on a wild ride? He lets us sink because He wants us to experience the reality of the principle found in Hebrews 12:2: "fixing our eyes on Jesus, the author and perfecter of faith."

Jesus is both the initiator and the fulfillment of our faith. He wants us to realize that He is both the start and the completion of all that we do. Following Jesus gets us out of the boat. But He is also the one who keeps us on top of the water.

Sometimes we step out in faith and then let our circumstances define us. We step out as we trust Jesus, but we sink because the situation consumes us. It drives us down and sucks us under.

"LORD, SAVE ME!"

When Peter saw that he was going down, he made a smart move. He cried out, "Lord, save me!" (Matthew 14:30).

And "immediately, Jesus stretched out His hand and took hold of him" (v. 31). The principle we get from Peter's experience on this stormy night is that when Peter regained his focus and put it back on Jesus Christ, he got pulled up and out of his sinking situation. When Peter took his eyes off of his circumstances and put them back on Christ, he was delivered from defeat. Our focus on Jesus isn't only needed to get us started; it is also the thing that will take us through our rock-and-a-hard-place times.

SAME SEA, DIFFERENT STORM

This is such an important point that I want to emphasize it by looking at another story about another storm. It's found earlier in Mark's narrative and begins, "On that day, when evening came, He said to them, 'Let us go over to the other side'" (Mark 4:35). Although Jesus is asking his disciples to cross the same Sea of Galilee, this time, He's going with them.

The story intensifies: "Leaving the crowd, they took Him along with them in the boat, just as He was; and other boats were with Him. And there arose a fierce gale of wind, and the waves were breaking over the boat so much that the boat was already filling up" (vv. 36–37).

A boat that is filling up with water is a death trap for fishermen. No doubt that panic filled the atmosphere around that boat. But when we read on we see that Jesus "was in the stern, asleep on the cushion" (v. 38).

Wait a minute. Let's get this straight. Jesus is in the same boat with them, and going through the same storm with them. They're panicking—and He's sleeping on a cushion! Whenever you're asleep on a pillow that means that you meant to go to sleep. If you've got a pillow tucked up under your head, then that's what I call on-purpose snoring.

DOES GOD CARE?

Jesus is sleeping on purpose not only in the middle of a storm, but in the middle of a storm so fierce that it is filling the boat up with water! Hello? Does this seem . . . normal?

The disciples don't think so. So they wake Him up. They ask, "Teacher, do you not care that we are perishing?" (v. 38).

Sometimes we're hard on the disciples and play armchair quarterback as we read their Bible stories, but this one seems like a fair question to me. We've all felt it at one time or another. We ask, "God, don't you even care? I'm on a wild ride in the middle of a fierce storm, caught between a rock and a hard place and you are off sleeping."

The disciples had raised a fundamental question, "Do you not care?" Jesus heard their question and woke up. He got up. Then He "rebuked the wind and said to the sea, 'Hush, be still'" (v. 39). The King James Version of the Bible says, "Peace, be still." Jesus told peace, or calm, to rule the situation. And it did.

We read, "And the wind died down and it became perfectly calm. And He said to them, 'Why are you so afraid? Do you still have no faith?'" (v. 39–40).

Look at Jesus' question again. He said, "Do you still have no faith?"

Let me be frank. I have a real problem with Jesus' question. From a human standpoint, that doesn't sound like an informed question. Maybe I'm being too transparent for my own good, but that question bothers me. Does it bother you?

I can see Pete, drenched to the bone, calmly saying, "Jesus, let me see if I understand: You are asking us why we lack faith? And, just be patient with me because I want to get this right. . . . Okay, Jesus, You are asking us why we are so timid?" Pete pauses. Jesus nods. Pete looks around at the boys. Then he continues, just as calmly as before, "I don't know, Jesus. Could it be because we are about to . . . DIE?!!!"

The boat is in the middle of the sea in the heart of a storm. Plus it's filling up with water. The thing is getting ready to sink! What kind of question is that?

Sometimes it doesn't seem like God is in tune with our situations, if the truth be told. I realize that writing those words is risky because people might think that I'm questioning whether God understands the situation, but give me a break! The ship is about to sink!

Tell the truth; you feel that way sometimes, too, don't you? Sometimes you just want to say, "You know what, God? You're off on this one. You're not quite up to snuff on what's going on with this one because this is a mess—and I'm afraid!"

If Jesus were in the hood, I'd be saying, "You cold, Jesus. You cold. You're not understanding my situation. What kind of question you be throwing down like that?"

How could Jesus say something that sounds so harsh?

One thing we know is that God always has a reason for what He does. And He's always right. Let's look at the passage again to find the answer to our concern. Because if we pay attention to verse 35, it says, "On that day, when evening came, He said to them, 'Let us go over to the other side.'"

LISTEN TO AND TRUST HIS WORDS

The answer to how Jesus could have asked such an apparently absurd question comes in this one short sentence, "Let us go over to the other side."

It will also help us to take a look at what Jesus didn't say in that sentence. Jesus didn't say, "Let's go halfway over, and then die." He also didn't say, "Let Me make it over all by Myself, and I hope you all get there somehow as well."

No; Jesus said, "Let us go over to the other side."

But even though He had said that, the disciples did what we often do when we go to church on Sundays, or when we are listening to sermons on the radio or reading books like this, and that is to say "Amen" without paying attention.

In other words, Jesus says, "Guys, I had told you that we were all going over to the other side. If you had listened to Me, then when you saw me sleeping on my pillow, you would have gotten your pillow, too. Because I had said that this is what we were going to do. But, no, you only heard My *words*. You didn't listen to My *voice*. And since this is true, the only way I know how to show you whether or not you were listening to me is by allowing something contrary to what I said take place."

Jesus wanted the disciples to see for themselves that they were not nearly as full of faith as they thought they were. He used the circumstances to prove it to them. Once the disciples saw Jesus calm the storm, though, their faith in Him grew. We read, "They became very much afraid and said to one another, 'Who then is this, that even the wind and the sea obey Him?'" (v. 41).

FEAR THE RIGHT THING

The disciples were still afraid just like they had been in the middle of the raging storm. Only now they feared the right thing—God, and not their circumstances.

This reminds me of a story about the woman who was driving down the highway when she spotted an eighteen-wheeler in her rearview mirror. It started to get too close for comfort, so she sped up. When she sped up, the driver sped up. She decided to exit the highway to lose him. So did he. And every turn that she would take, he would take. Finally, she was getting terrified because he kept following her.

The woman then sped into a filling station parking lot, jumped out of her car, and ran into the mart. The truck driver also pulled into the gas station. She watched as the man stopped his rig, jumped out of the cab, came down . . . and raced over to the backseat of her car. He then jerked the door open and yanked out a man he had seen sneak into her car earlier when she did not realize it.

All along, the person the woman had thought had been trying to hurt her had actually been the savior pursuing her. Yet because she didn't have all of the information, she feared the wrong thing.

Sometimes we end up fearing the wrong thing, too. We look at our circumstances and it appears that they are against us, when actually it is our Savior pursuing us to rid us of harmful things that we can't see. As well as to give us an experience of His delivering power that we wouldn't normally have had.

FAITH AT A DEEPER LEVEL

God knows that we need to experience Him at a deeper level for our faith to grow. But sometimes it even requires multiple snags between rocks and hard places for that to happen. Just like with the disciples.

We see an example of this when we return to the story of Jesus walking on the water in Mark 6. We read, "But immediately [Jesus] spoke with them and said to them, 'Take courage; it is I, do not be afraid.' Then He got into the boat with them, and the wind stopped" (vv. 50–51).

Once again, Jesus calmed them down internally with the Word. "Take courage," he said. He addressed their internal chaos before joining them to address their external problem. The internal was calmed by His Word, but the external was calmed when Jesus joined them in the boat.

WHY SUCH HARD HEARTS?

Once things were calm, we read that the disciples "were utterly astonished." They were mesmerized and shocked. Why? Because "they had not gained any insight from the incident of the loaves, but their heart was hardened" (vv. 51–52).

A heart has only two options. It can soften. Or it can harden. It cannot just be neutral. How the disciples managed to get through the miracle of the feeding of the five thousand and not gain any insight from it could have only happened with hardened hearts. But why were their hearts so hardened?

Taking a closer look at the story of the loaves and fish earlier in Mark 6 (vv. 33–44 and as recounted in John 6:1–13) will reveal the reason. Because in this story we witness the power of God. But it is the power of God meeting someone else's felt need.

The skinny on the story goes like this: There are five thousand men, not counting women and children, listening to Jesus teach. So there are probably twenty thousand people altogether. It's lunchtime. Jesus wants to know, "How are we going to feed all of these people?"

Philip answers, essentially, "Jesus, I don't have the slightest idea. We don't have enough money to feed the thirteen of us, let alone twenty thousand." So Jesus skips Philip. He's obviously no help. He doesn't get it. Jesus turns his attention to Andrew instead. Andrew's at least trying. Andrew says, "Jesus, I don't know what to do. There's nothing out here. All I've got is a boy with two fish and five barley loaves. It's just a handful of sardines and crackers. Do you want them or not, Jesus?" (That's my paraphrase of John 6:5–9.)

Sardines and crackers. That doesn't even sound like enough to feed the kid. But Jesus said, "Bring him to me."

Andrew took the little boy's lunch to Jesus. Then Jesus commanded them to sit down in groups on the grass. Mark 6:41 says that "He took the five loaves and the two fish, and looking up toward heaven, He blessed the food."

GIVE THANKS FOR WHAT GOD GIVES

Now wait a minute. Jesus just blessed a couple of fish and a few loaves of bread? He blessed a little boy's lunch? Doesn't that seem like that's not very much for which to give thanks? It does to me. We've got twenty thousand people out here tired and hungry, and we're going to give thanks for some sardines and crackers? Come on. You're asking me to give thanks for what is an apparent insufficiency? You're asking me to give thanks for what is clearly not enough?

But Jesus blessed it and gave thanks. In doing that, He gave us a principle for when we find ourselves in a situation where there clearly isn't enough. Maybe we don't have enough money, time, energy, willpower, health, or opportunity. Whatever the situation, Jesus showed us what to do when we don't have enough to meet a need, yet the need still must be met: Thank God for what He does give to us.

Jesus blessed the food. In John's rendering of the story, we read that Jesus gave thanks. Jesus gave thanks for not enough. In essence, He said, "Lord, I thank You that even though we do not have enough, I want to thank You for what You have provided. In thanking You, I am trusting You to turn 'not enough' into 'more than enough.'"

The next part of Mark 6:41 says that after He blessed it, He "broke the loaves and He kept giving them to the disciples to set before [the people]."

Watch this: Jesus prays, gives thanks, and blesses some sardines and crackers. Then, out of nowhere, Moby Dick lands on the beach. Either that or it's Orca the killer whale, because whatever it is, it's huge. The disciples keep breaking it off and giving it to the people.

The people ate and they were satisfied. Then the disciples picked up twelve baskets of broken pieces of bread and fish—leftovers! This is after perhaps twenty thousand people had eaten and were satisfied. To be satisfied is not to eat the small portions you get when you buy a lean-watch-your-weight kind of dinner in the frozen food section of the grocery store. For them to be satisfied when they ate means they ate more than enough.

The tendency is to whine rather than to bless. The tendency is to bail out on God rather than to turn to Him. But when you give thanks for your insufficiency, God can turn your "not enough" into "more than enough."

Habakkuk is my hero because he learned to praise God in a praiseless situation. Habakkuk spends most of his book saying things like, "God, I don't know what You're doing. I don't understand how You're doing it. You're making no sense to me. I'm frustrated, aggravated, and irritated." But then, after all of that, Habakkuk says, in essence, "God, in spite of what I don't understand and though it seems like You are just messing me over, I will praise You."

The final verses of Habakkuk 3 capture the prophet's faith:

> Though the fig tree should not blossom and there be no fruit on the vines, though the yield of the olive should fail and the fields produce no food, though the flock should be cut off from the fold and there be no cattle in the stalls, yet I will exult in the Lord, I will rejoice in the God of my salvation. The Lord God is my strength, and He has made my feet like hinds' feet, and makes me walk on my high places. (vv. 17–19)

The reason why anyone would want hinds' feet is because these are the feet of mountain deer, and they can both climb mountains and scale rough terrain. Habakkuk rejoices in God because even though he is between a rock and a hard place, he knows that God has given him the ability to climb up and out of whatever situation he is in. Habakkuk doesn't know how God will do it, and he doesn't know when God will do it. But he knows that God has enabled him to maneuver through it. And so Habakkuk praises God in a praiseless situation.

CHOOSING TO HAVE
GRATEFUL—OR HARDENED—HEARTS

I know at times you want to give up. I know at times you are in a dry and thirsty land. But you and I must remind ourselves to hope in God. We can still praise Him if we have hope in God. God will meet us not only in the midst of "not enough" and in the middle of the storm, He will gives us "more than enough." And as he did with the disciples, He then will throw in peace as a bonus.

But He also wants to see what you learned from it when He does it. We can have grateful, expectant hearts, or we can let our hearts harden and our faith waiver. Right after ("immediately," Mark 6:45 says) they had seen what God could do in feeding a huge crowd with a boy's small lunch, God put them in a scenario to see if they had really believed what they saw God do. They had seen God provide food for twenty thousand hungry stomachs. But now that they were in distress, would they trust God for their own need? No, for they hadn't yet learned to be confident in a God who transcends sensory limitations. They wouldn't learn this until God was all they had in whom to be confident.

It's easy for followers of Jesus to say "Amen" when we trust God will supply for someone else, but it's more difficult when it's you or I who has lost a job, a home, or personal health, and we need to trust God to meet our needs. Will you and I remain grateful and faithful then?

SEEING GOD OURSELVES

John reveals the disciples' response to Jesus' calling out to them from on top of the water. As I mentioned at the beginning of this chapter, Matthew, Mark, and Luke often tell the same stories. John is not included in the Synoptic Gospels because he rarely repeats any of the other Gospel writers' stories. His account is written to show the uniqueness of the Person and works of Jesus Christ unto salvation. But John does recount the miracle of Jesus walking on the water.

And in his account, John tells something that none of the other three Gospel writers include: "But He said to them, 'It is I; do not be afraid.' So they were willing to receive Him into the boat" (John 6:20–21). Through John's Gospel, we learn why Jesus got into the boat; the disciples were "willing to receive Him." Just like what happened on the road to Emmaus, they were willing to receive Him into their contradictory situation.

When they received Him, things changed. John tells us, "And *immediately* the boat was at the land to which they were going" (v. 21, italics added).

It's only one word but it's swollen with truth; it says "immediately." Now, last time I checked, the boat was in the middle of the sea, about four miles from shore. Last time I checked, the disciples were debating whether to turn back or to press on. They were between a rock and a hard place. Should we keep going? Or should we go back?

But Jesus called to them and calmed the storm inside. When He did, they saw Him for themselves. They saw Him in the middle of their need, their pain, and their contradiction. When they heard His voice, they received Him. When they received Him, a miraculous thing happened: Four miles of water suddenly became nothing. The distance between where they were and where they needed to be was supernaturally closed simply because Jesus was received into the boat.

FROM DISASTER TO MIRACLE WITH JESUS

I want you to know that Jesus can do all of these things that we have looked at in the last few chapters for you, too. If you will receive Him in the middle of your contradictions and in your trick bag, He can take a storm and turn it into peace. When Jesus shows up in your messed-up situation, things change. When Jesus shows up in your stressed-filled, jacked-up scenario, ground gets covered quickly. When Jesus shows up—not simply because you hear His Word but because you receive His Person—He can close the gap of time, the gap of a situation, the gap of not enough and the gap of resistance. Jesus can immediately turn what looked like certain disaster into a supernatural miracle.

The principle is this: When you're between a rock and a hard place or out in the middle of a storm with darkness all around you, receive Jesus into your situation. He will join you. Not only will He join you, but He can get you where you needed to go all along.

What's best about that is that He can do it immediately. If He can cross four miles of sea in a wooden boat in less time than it would take to stick an oar in the water, then He can easily handle where He's taking you.

When you hear His voice in the middle of your mess, receive Him. He wants to join you. He's just waiting to see what you are going to do.

IN THE HARD PLACES

1. "Why does [Jesus] let us sink . . . when we've stepped out in faith?" Pastor Evans asks (see "Into the Water"). How does Pastor Evans answer the question? Do you agree?

2. During an earlier crossing of a turbulent Sea of Galilee when Jesus was with them, the disciples found Jesus sleeping during a storm. How did they react (Mark 4:38)? After calming the storm, how did Jesus react to their fear (v. 40)? What *healthy* fear did they develop by watching Jesus, according to verse 41?

3. Before the second crossing of the Sea of Galilee, the disciples had watched Jesus' miraculous feeding of five thousand men. Yet when it came to their own great need, they had not learned to be confident in God. Mark says "their heart was hardened" (6:52). Why do we often forget who God is and lack expectant hearts?

4. In the final three paragraphs, Pastor Evans gives a principle that can turn a "certain disaster" into deliverance. What is the principle? Why do you think it is difficult for so many followers of Jesus to act on this principle?

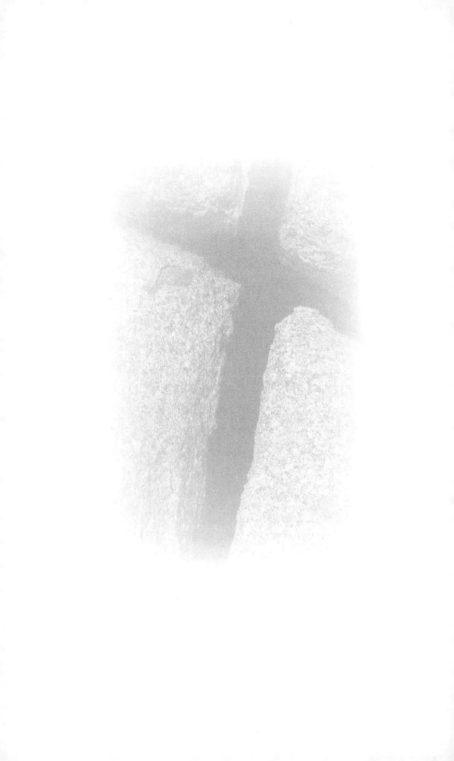

7

Martha, Mary, and Lazarus

WHEN GOD LETS YOU DOWN

WHEN THE HEAD COACH of an NFL team believes that a referee has made a wrong call, awarding a key play to the opposition, he throws a red flag on the ground. This flag signals that the referee needs to review the play again. Obviously the coach believes that the referee has made a mistake.

In our lives there are times, especially when we are caught between a rock and a hard place, when we want to throw a red flag out on God. We want to toss the flag and stop the game because it looks like God has made a wrong call. We think He has missed something. We think He didn't know what He was doing because if He did, He wouldn't have called things that way.

We think thoughts like, *If God had known how this was going to affect me, He wouldn't have allowed that thing to happen. If He had really known the pain that I would experience in dealing with this, He would have made a different decision.*

We want to reach into our pocket and pull out our red flag and yell, "God, you missed this one! You blew it. Review it, because you're obviously wrong."

In John 11, two sisters throw a red flag on God after their brother becomes gravely ill. Martha and Mary had sent word to Jesus to come and to heal their brother, Lazarus. We read:

> Now a certain man was sick, Lazarus of Bethany, the village of Mary and her sister Martha. It was the Mary who anointed the Lord with ointment, and wiped His feet with her hair, whose brother Lazarus was sick. So the sisters sent word to Him, saying, "Lord, behold, he whom You love is sick." But when Jesus heard this, He said, "This sickness is not to end in death, but for the glory of God, so that the Son of God may be glorified by it." Now Jesus loved Martha and her sister and Lazarus. (vv. 1–5)

Martha and Mary started out in their soon-to-be a rock-and-a-hard-place situation by doing the right thing. They took their problem to Jesus.

From the passage we learn that Lazarus and his sisters had a special relationship with Jesus. The sisters had said, "Lord, behold, he whom You love is sick." We're not talking about somebody who doesn't care about spiritual things or has no relationship with Jesus. We're talking about somebody whom Jesus loves. In verse 5, we learn Jesus cared deeply for Lazarus' two sisters as well. Jesus had shared a frequent and unique fellowship with all three of them.

Notice that Jesus immediately gave them hope. He sent back a word of expectation, saying, "This sickness is not to end in death." Martha and Mary heard the comforting reassurances that "It's going to be all right. It's not as bad as it seems. God is going to be glorified. Relax."

So far, so good. Lazarus gets sick. Martha and Mary send word to their close friend and miracle maker, Jesus. Jesus sends word back telling them not to worry because all is well.

The problem comes, though, when Lazarus dies.

THE VOLATILE EMOTIONS OF A MAJOR LOSS

After having done the right thing and receiving hope from Jesus' word, the two sisters watch things get worse for Lazarus. When Martha and Mary had started this pilgrimage, Lazarus was sick. Then he got sicker. Now Lazarus is dead.

Have you ever experienced something like this? Have you ever been in a situation when things fell apart *after* you went to Jesus? Have you ever experienced a death? Not just a physical death, because death is essentially a loss. Have you ever experienced a deep loss of any kind? Maybe it was (or is) a loss of your dreams, hopes, relationships, career, family, finances, or your health. Stuff started to get sick, and then it just died. You had this plan for your life. You had a hope. You thought that things were going to fall right into place. But not only did they not fall into place, they died.

If you have ever been in a situation like that, then you know exactly what Martha and Mary were experiencing when they got caught between a rock and a hard place. They experienced contradictory and volatile emotions. Lazarus is sick. Martha and Mary reach out to Jesus for help. Jesus sends back hope. Lazarus dies.

WHEN JESUS DOES NOT COME . . .

Then, after Lazarus dies, Jesus has the seeming audacity to tell his disciples, "Lazarus is dead, and I am glad for your sakes that I was not there" (vv. 14–15).

. . . SHOCK

Hold up. Jesus didn't just say that, did He? It's bad enough for Jesus not to make it a priority to come to his friends in their time of need, but then to say that He's glad that He wasn't even there? If Martha and Mary got wind of Jesus' talk, they might have said, "What? We called you. We needed you. We trusted You. You loved us. We were in pain. You had the ability to ease that pain. And You spread it around to your homeboys that You are glad that You weren't even here! Come on, Jesus, what kind of friend is that?"

If that isn't enough to rip a heart in two, there's more. John reports that "when [Jesus] heard that he was sick, He then stayed two days longer in the place where He was" (v. 6). Jesus knew that Martha and Mary needed Him, and yet He delayed. You would have thought that given the fact that He loved them, He would have hurried up and gone to their aid. But He did just the opposite. Jesus intentionally delayed responding to a disaster in the lives of three people whom He loved.

The trip He had needed to take in order to reach them wasn't all that long. John tells us that Jesus had been only two miles away (v. 18). That's just a morning's walk. He was only two miles away from fixing their problem. He was only two miles from solving their dilemma. He was only two miles from bringing calm to their chaos. Jesus was up the road and had plenty of time to come. He just didn't.

Maybe you have been in a sickening situation like Martha,

Mary, and Lazarus at one point in your life. Maybe you have called out to Jesus, but He didn't come. Maybe you are there right now. Things seem to be going from bad to worse. You love Jesus. Jesus loves you. You call out to Jesus but He doesn't come through.

If you are in a situation like that right now, I want to remind you that you are more in God's will now than you have ever been in your life.

In Lazarus' scenario, we have Jesus loving Lazarus and Lazarus loving Jesus. We have people praying; Martha and Mary are calling out to Jesus. In God's sovereignty, His Son chooses to delay.

. . . DISAPPOINTMENT AND FRUSTRATION

But this, brothers and sisters, can lead to disappointment with God.

Maybe you know what it is like to feel disappointed with God. I'm not going to pretend to be super spiritual and deny that I do. I've been disappointed with God. I imagine that you have, too. You get disappointed with God when He doesn't come through for you; and on top of that, He doesn't even tell you why He's not coming through for you.

That makes you disappointed. That makes you frustrated. You start wondering what's the use of being a Christian when you are in a rock-and-a-hard-place situation and you call on Jesus only to have Jesus delay.

GOD'S UNKNOWN BUT GREATER PURPOSE

If you are in a situation like that right now, I want to encourage you not to give up. If you are disappointed with God right now, I want to remind you that He knows your name. He cares for you.

If you can't see God coming through for you right now even

though you are doing everything you know to do during a tough situation, don't throw in the towel just yet. Because when God delays, He always delays for a greater purpose. You might not be able to see that purpose right now because you live within the confines of linear time. But God knows what's just around the corner. And it's worth the wait.

DEATH AS SLEEP

Jesus, always capitalizing on a moment, turns His delay into a teaching time for His disciples. "Our friend Lazarus has fallen asleep; but I go, so that I may awaken him out of sleep" (v. 11). In Jesus' delay, He introduces a new concept to them: sleep.

The word *sleep* is only used of believers in the New Testament when they die. Instead of viewing death as a cessation of existence, Jesus illustrates it as merely a transfer of consciousness, like sleep. When you are asleep, you are still very much alive.

Most of us do not fear going to sleep. In fact, most of us probably look forward to going to sleep. The reason why we are not afraid to go to sleep is because we know that all we are doing is transitioning into another arena of awareness. By sleeping, we are not ceasing to exist.

As a believer, you don't even get to die. So if you fear death, then you fear something that will never happen. Because to fear death as a believer is akin to fearing going to sleep. The Bible says, "We are confident, I say, and willing rather to be absent from the body, and to be present with the Lord" (2 Corinthians 5:8 KJV). When you die, you won't be dead long enough to even know that you died. There is an immediate transition into the presence of God.

Jesus uses the word *sleep* when talking about Lazarus' death because He wants the disciples—and all of us—to look at things through spiritual eyes. He doesn't want us to see things through the eyes of the same limited physical world that defines our existence day by day. When we are too tied to the physical realm and definitions, we miss out on spiritual potentialities. Jesus wants us to view life through spiritual eyes.

The disciples don't get this new truth. Instead they told Jesus, "Lord, if he has fallen asleep, he will recover" (v. 12). They are still thinking of sleep in the normal sense of the word.

When Jesus hears their literal interpretation of "sleep," He speaks bluntly: "Lazarus is dead . . . let us go to him" (vv.14–15).

THROWING THE RED FLAG

Jesus eventually reaches the outskirts of the village, where Martha spots Him. Martha and Mary will see Jesus at different times and in different locations, but they both will greet Him by saying the exact same thing: "Lord, if You had been here, my brother would not have died" (vv. 21, 32). The first words out of both Martha's and Mary's mouths when Jesus comes are essentially, "Jesus, this is Your fault. Because if You would have been here, we wouldn't be here. We wouldn't be dealing with sickness, loss, death, and emotional pain."

The unspoken question through all of their words is: What good is a God who isn't there when you need Him the most?

That is an understandable question in light of what has just happened. It's okay to admit that you've thought the same thoughts or had the same questions. I have. How about if we give ourselves permission to not sugarcoat our faith and act like everything is all good, all the time? Because it's not. For us to say that it would be lying. Lying is a sin.

So let's get real, like Martha and Mary. Sometimes we just want to shout, "Jesus, this is Your bad! You let me down!" We throw out the red flag.

There are many different ways that we can do that. Martha and Mary illustrate two of them for us. "Martha therefore, when she heard that Jesus was coming, went to meet Him, but Mary stayed at the house" (v. 20).

These two sisters have distinct personality types. Martha is vocal and confrontational. She will get all up in your face, if she feels like she needs to do that. When Jesus had visited their home much earlier for dinner, Martha had a big, fancy display for Jesus and his disciples. Mary settled down in the den near Jesus and shared some conversation with Him, leaving Martha to do all of the work. Martha got ticked off when she came out to the den and saw Mary fraternizing with Jesus instead of helping out in the hot kitchen cooking all of the food for all of those hungry preachers. We read:

> Martha was distracted with all her preparations; and she came up to Him and said, "Lord, do You not care that my sister has left me to do all the serving alone? Then tell her to help me." But the Lord answered and said to her, "Martha, Martha, you are worried and bothered about so many things; but only one thing is necessary, for Mary has chosen the good part, which shall not be taken away from her." (Luke 10:40–42)

Essentially, Martha huffed over to Jesus and asked, "Jesus, will you tell Mary to come and help me because she has left the whole kitchen to me all by myself. And that's just not right, Jesus. That's not right."

Jesus told her, "Hush your fuss, Martha. I'll do no such thing. Your problem is that you have too much going on at one time.

A casserole will do. One thing will do. Mary has chosen the better way."

We see from the story that Martha is the outspoken one who will confront you. Mary, on the other hand, is the quiet one. Because these two sisters are so different, when Jesus arrives on the scene of Lazarus' death, we hear the same words but witness two dissimilar deliveries. Both of the sisters are disappointed. I know that because they both say the same thing. But Martha bolts out of the door of the house, runs down the road, and immediately confronts Jesus.

On the other hand, Mary is so upset that she won't even leave the house. Mary stays home. Martha races down the road while Mary says, "I'm not talking to Him. If He wants to talk to me, He can come to me. Because all of this is His fault."

Whatever our personality types—whether the outward, go-to-God-face-to-face type, the inward, don't-want-to-talk-about-it type, or something else—we can be assured that Jesus will meet us where we are.

WHAT MARTHA KNEW

Martha wastes no time at all when Jesus arrives; she wants to go deep, quickly. After declaring, "'Lord, if You had been here, my brother would not have died," she throws out a theological statement that has staggering implications: "Even now I know that whatever You ask of God, God will give You" (John 11:21–22).

It's easy to read over that statement and miss it. Martha is in a hopeless situation—I'm talking death here. Even so, she says that she knows something. She reaches back to what she knows to be true in spite of the circumstances that she is in. *She knows that whatever Jesus asks His Father to do, He will do.*

That is one of the most profound truths you will ever discover. We will look at it more closely in the next chapter, but I want you to get this now. Whatever Jesus asks of the Father, the Father does. The Father never turns down the Son except when the Son died on the cross, because there was sin involved in that situation. But other than that one unique time, the Father never turns down the Son. And Martha knows that.

A PERSONAL WORD FROM JESUS

Jesus replies to her faith by saying, "Your brother will rise again" (v. 23).

Watch what just happened. Martha laid out a general theological truth: "What You ask of the Father, the Father will do." Her general theological truth then leads her to a personal word from Jesus: "Your brother will rise again."

In Jesus' affirming of her objective truth, He gives her a personal word about her brother. Jesus personalized his communication with her when she affirmed His general truth. In other words, if you do not believe in His general revelation, He's not going to give you specific application. But because Martha affirmed general revelation, He gave her specific application. Then, if we peek ahead at verse 25, we will see that when she wanted clarification on the application that came from the revelation, Jesus Christ gave her Himself. He revealed, "I am the resurrection and the life."

The great problem we often find in our churches today is that people can come to church and get revelation without leaving the church and having personal application. You just heard it, nodded with it, or said "Amen" to it. But unless you receive it, you will never get a specific application, like Martha did. In order to hear the "secret" things of God that are personal with our names on them, we must first believe and act on the general revelation that He has given. Abraham, sacrifice your son. Moses, remove your shoes. Disciples, cross the sea.

When Martha gets this personal word that her brother will rise again, she makes a deeper theological declaration: "I know that he will rise again in the resurrection on the last day'" (v. 24).

Martha says, to all intents and purposes, "Jesus, I got that already. I know the eschatological program that You are talking about. But that's not what I'm talking about. I'm talking about my disappointment now. I need a solution now because I'm between a rock and a hard place now."

JESUS, THE RIGHT-NOW GOD

Jesus then answers by throwing in a zinger. He says, "I am the resurrection and the life; he who believes in Me will live even if he dies, and everyone who lives and believes in Me will never die" (vv. 25–26).

Why is that a zinger? Because Jesus says that until you turn your theology about me into an experience with me, it will remain doctrine on paper and not a reality in your existence.

Martha has the right theology. She says, "I know he will rise again." Martha is saying that her theology tells her that he will rise again in the last day. But Jesus responded, "I *am* the resurrection and the life" (italics added). Christ is saying while her brother will rise in the future, Christ is also a right-now God in the middle of a dead situation. Jesus wants Martha to know that not only will He be the resurrection in the future, but He is also a resurrecting God right now.

Once He makes that clear, Jesus tags on a question. He asks her, "Do you believe this?" (v. 26). Jesus wants to know if she not only believes her theology, which is correct, but if she also believes that He is who He says He is right now. Not just for the future in anticipation, but for now. Does she believe His personal revelation?

That's a question that He asks us, too. You can believe all of the theological truth that you were taught but not experience its relevancy in your life right now. God doesn't just want a relationship with us where we can spout theology. He wants a relationship with us where we've seen theology come alive in our experiences. He wants the truth about God to become an "I Am" reality. That's what He was saying to Martha.

God often will allow truth about Himself to lead us into an intimate experience with Him because truth alone, without the Person, is just a cognitive understanding without power. God lets us get stuck between a rock and a hard place for a reason. God lets things die in your life and mine for the express purpose of letting us witness what He can do when we believe that He is the I Am not just for our tomorrow, but also for our today.

IN THE HARD PLACES

1. "You get disappointed with God when He doesn't come through for you." Or you may feel frustrated, even shocked. Which of these emotions have you experienced when you felt God ignored you or your prayers? Is it okay to feel this way? Why or why not?

2. What did Martha know about Jesus' relationship with God the Father? Despite this profound theological truth, Martha still was sad that Jesus had not come earlier. What does this tell you about the struggles among theological truth, feelings, and faith?

3. Jesus responded to Martha's general theological truth with a personal word: "Your brother will rise again." What happened to Martha—and will happen to us—when she affirmed general revelation?

4. How is Jesus a right-now God and "not just a tomorrow God"? Why is it important that we have "a right-now God in the middle of a dead situation?"

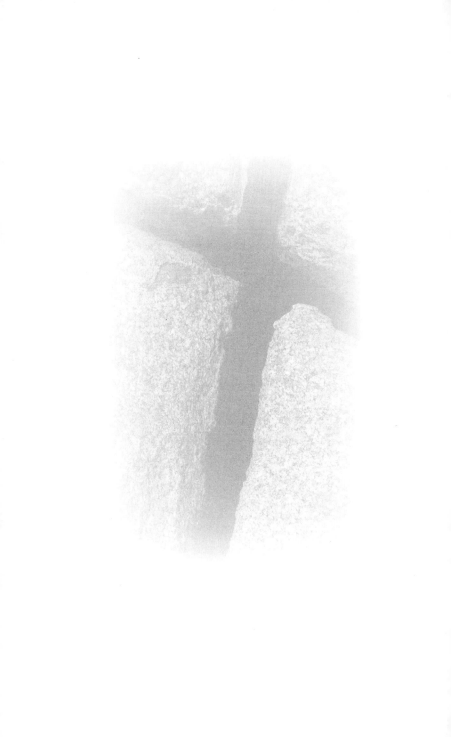

8

Martha, Mary & Lazarus

REMOVE THE STONE

WE BEGIN OUR LAST CHAPTER on the subject of when God puts you between a rock and a hard place with the shortest verse in the Bible. It's amazing how something so small can say so much. This verse is just two words. But I don't want us to lose the meaning of this verse just because of its length.

"Jesus wept," the apostle John tells us (11:35).

Martha had told Jesus that she believed He was the resurrection and the life (v. 27). She had then run to tell Mary that Jesus had come.

Now Mary, seeing Jesus, falls at His feet and says, "Lord, if You had been here, my brother would not have died" (v. 32). John reports that when Jesus "saw her weeping, and the Jews who came with her also weeping, He was deeply moved in spirit and was troubled, and said, 'Where have you laid him?' They said to Him, 'Lord, come and see'" (vv. 33–34).

Then, John writes, "Jesus wept."

JESUS FEELS OUR PAIN

There is a lot of crying going on here. Martha is crying. Mary is crying. The Jews are crying. Seeing the agitated emotions all around Him, Jesus is "moved in His spirit and deeply troubled." Jesus felt Mary's pain.

The beautiful thing about Jesus is that He knows how you feel. Jesus can identify with your pain because He was a man. He knows what it is like to lose those He loves. He knows what it is like to be rejected. He knows what it is like for birds to have nests and foxes to have dens, but for the Son of Man to have no place to lay his head (Matthew 8:20). Jesus knows what it is to be hungry. He knows what it is to be thirsty. He knows what it is to grieve. Jesus not only knows how you feel, but He also sees your tears, and cries with you.

"Jesus wept."

Don't miss the meaning in those two words. Don't ever forget that no tear you cry goes without His notice and also His empathy. Jesus wept. He wept with Mary. He weeps with you, too. Remember that.

A REQUEST THAT MAKES NO SENSE

The next part of the passage contains potentially the most revolutionary spiritual truth you could ever learn for your daily living. It can sustain you when you're caught between a rock and a hard place. We read: "So Jesus, again being deeply moved within, came to the tomb. Now it was a cave, and a stone was lying against it. Jesus said, 'Remove the stone.' Martha, the sister of the deceased, said to Him, 'Lord, by this time there will be a stench, for he has been dead four days'" (vv. 38–39).

Jesus makes a simple request, "Remove the stone." Martha interrupts to let Jesus know that what He is asking isn't practical. She lets Jesus know that what He is asking isn't logical. It makes no biological sense.

"My brother has been dead for four days now," Martha explains. "Do you remember that delay that you did, Jesus? When someone has been dead for four days, there is bodily decay. That means there is going to be a stench. If You would have been here, he wouldn't be in this situation. But now that You are here, I don't think removing the stone is our best option."

When God puts you or me between a rock and a hard place, He will often make a request that makes absolutely no sense. His request to the mourners is not logical. Lazarus is literally between a rock and a hard place. Lazarus is literally behind a stone. Jesus asks the mourners to remove the stone without giving them any more information.

Here's the spiritual truth you can apply to your daily life: When God is getting ready to do something significant in your life that involves a deliverance from a situation gone bad, or a resurrection of a situation that has died, it will often include an illogical request. This request makes no practical sense to Martha. But neither do many of the requests that we have seen in our previous chapters. Abraham is told to sacrifice his son, and yet his son is going to be the head of a great nation. Moses is told to hold his shepherd's staff out over a huge body of water so that God will then part it and turn it into dry land. Peter is told to step out of the boat in the middle of a storm on top of the water and start walking. None of those requests seems logical.

Whenever God is getting ready to do something in your rock-and-a-hard-place situation, don't be surprised if He gives you a request that doesn't make sense. And I want to encourage you, when that happens, don't go logical on God. What we often do with God in situations like that is debate the instruction. Just like Martha did. Last time I checked, Jesus' instruction to her was pretty simple, "Remove the stone." He wasn't asking her to do rocket science. He just said, "Remove the stone."

This reminds me of something that comes up frequently in the middle of counseling sessions that I hold at our church. After hearing an issue, I will then present God's view, His revealed will through His Word, on that issue to whomever I am counseling. Often I will then get a logical reason why that won't work. I have just presented what the Bible says on the matter. I will get back a well-organized, documented reason why that won't work. Inevitably when this occurs, I feel like asking what would have happened to Joshua and the Israelites if they would have done the same thing? What would have happened if Joshua would have said, "That's a nice word from You, God, but that's not going to work."

JOSHUA'S CHALLENGE TO OBEY

Picture Joshua with me for a moment.

Joshua is the commander of the Israelite army. He has experience in leading wars. God says to him, "Joshua, here is your divine military strategy straight from the top. I want you to walk all the way around Jericho once a day for six days. On the seventh day, I want you and everyone with you to walk around that wall seven times. On the seventh time—now pay attention, because here is the clincher—I want everybody to *scream*. How about that?"

Joshua is facing a battle against a walled city. Defenders are sitting on top of the wall, armed with bows, arrows, and spears pointed right at his army. Joshua's soldiers have no defense walking around that wall. That's not logical. Neither is it logical to think that you will tear down a fortified wall that has stood there for years just by screaming. But with God, it's not about logic. That's the point. It's about doing what He says to do in faith.

Joshua did what God said, and on the seventh day we read, "The people shouted with a great shout and the wall fell down flat" (Joshua 6:20).

CAPTAIN NAAMAN'S CHALLENGE

Or what about Naaman? Naaman was a captain in the army of Aram who was plagued with leprosy. Naaman had heard about the prophet Elisha, so he went to see if Elisha could heal him. Elisha, on the other hand, didn't even come to the door but sent the maid instead. She told Naaman, "Go and wash in the Jordan seven times, and your flesh will be restored to you and you will be clean" (2 Kings 5:10).

Naaman got offended at this. He got so mad that he stomped off without any intention of following the instructions that he had received. We read,

> But Naaman was furious and went away and said, "Behold, I thought, 'He will surely come out to me and stand and call on the name of the Lord his God, and wave his hand over the place and cure the leper.' Are not Abanah and Pharpar, the rivers of Damascus, better than all the waters of Israel? Could I not wash in them and be clean?" So he turned and went away in a rage. (2 Kings 5:11–12)

Naaman gave up because the instructions seemed absurd. First, he was taken aback that Elisha didn't even bother to talk to him in person. Then his logic kicked in and he argued that the rivers of Damascus were cleaner than the Jordan. He checked out of the plan because he didn't have time for such a makeshift solution to his problem. But while he was leaving, his servants chased him down and said, "My father, had the prophet told you to do some great thing, would you not have done it? How much more then, when he says to you, 'Wash, and be clean'?" (v. 13).

Finally, Naaman agreed. "He went down and dipped himself seven times in the Jordan, according to the word of the man of God; and his flesh was restored like the flesh of a little child and he was clean" (v. 14).

Many scenarios in the Bible displaying God's divine intervention came with a request that didn't make sense. Once you add human logic to the Word of God, you ignore the power of the Word of God in your situation. The moment God says one thing, and you say, "Wait, but, I think . . ." you have just canceled what God has said.

PULLING BACK ON THE REINS OF LOGIC

When I was learning to ride a horse at a family camp in eastern Texas with my son, I thought that I knew the basics of horseback riding. I had seen the TV shows *Gunsmoke* and *Wyatt Earp*. I figured that I knew everything there was to know about riding a horse. How hard could it be? You climb on, make a clicking noise with your mouth, say "Giddyup," and kick the horse on its side.

That's what I did. But something was wrong with my horse. I had a disturbed horse. It was an afflicted horse. Because every time I would say "Giddyup" and kick it on its side, my horse would go forward and then start backing up.

I quickly called the wrangler over because I wanted a new horse. I told him that I had a crazy horse. The wrangler took one look at what I was doing and told me that it wasn't my horse that was the crazy one. He told me that my horse was confused because I was saying "Giddyup" and kicking it on its side, while at the same time pulling back on the reins.

"You can't do that, Tony," he said. "You have confused this animal. It doesn't know which way to go."

A lot of us do the same thing with God. On Sunday, we shout, "Praise the Lord, giddyup, God; ride on, King Jesus"; yet at the same time we are pulling back on the reins of human logic. Then we wonder why we don't see deliverance from our rock-and-a-hard-place situation. We don't see deliverance because Jesus said, "Remove the stone," and we say, "Wait, that doesn't make sense."

Jesus doesn't want to have a discussion about the stone He has told us to remove. He doesn't want to know how big the stone is. He doesn't want to know how long the stone has been there. He doesn't even want to know how dead the dead is behind the stone. All Jesus wants you to do is remove the stone.

After Martha's argument, it sounds like Jesus is getting annoyed. He replies, "Did I not say to you that if you believe, you will see the glory of God?" (John 11:40).

FROM DISCUSSION TO DELIVERANCE

Jesus sounds like a parent here, "Didn't you hear what I said? Were you not paying attention? I said, 'Remove the stone,' and you want to have a discussion about the aspects of death. You want to talk about how bodies rot. You want to get into this long discussion and inform the omniscient one who already knows all things. Did I not say?"

A lot of us, like Martha, are delaying our deliverance by discussion. We're spending so much time discussing how illogical the expectations of God are that we can't get around to deliverance. So we find our situation stuck in a grave.

Jesus said, "Did I not say?" He is reminding Martha about their conversation that they had just had. He's reminding her of the theological discussion that had already taken place. They didn't need to have another one. Earlier he had told her, "'I am the resurrection and the life; he who believes in Me will live even if he dies, and everyone who lives and believes in Me will never die. Do you believe this?'" (vv. 25–26).

Martha had gotten very spiritual during that interchange. She had said, "Sure, Jesus, I believe it. I trust You. You're the wheel in the middle of a wheel. You're the Rose of Sharon. You're all that, and more. I believe, Jesus!"

"Okay, then," said Jesus. "Have them remove the stone."

"Wait," said Martha, "let's talk."

The problem is that Martha went no further than the biblical truth that she had learned about but had never needed to apply. The theological information was good for a classroom and good for notes in her notebook, but she never had needed to use it in her life. Now she did.

We are a lot like Martha. We believe in a Jesus that we can talk about, but not a Jesus that we know much about personally. We believe that He can reverse things for others; He just can't do it for me.

Jesus said it as plainly as He could: "Did I not say to you that if you believe, you will see the glory of God?" (v. 40). This is another one of those nuggets that we find in the Bible. Don't misread that verse. Jesus didn't say, "If you see, Martha, you will believe." He said, "If you believe, you will see."

LIVE BY FAITH

Here's the principle: To experience the living Christ in your dead situation, belief must precede sight, because without faith it is impossible to please God (Hebrews 11:6). Faith precedes sight. One of the great verses in the Bible describes this situation. It says, "Now faith is the assurance of things hoped for, the conviction of things not seen" (11:1). In other words, belief requires no empirical evidence to validate what you are doing. There is nothing to taste, smell, touch, hear, or see in order for you to believe. There is nothing that the five senses can grab because if there is, then that is no longer faith. You don't have to see something to know that it's real. But what you do have to do is act in faith.

God says that the righteous "shall live by faith" (10:38). So how do you know when you have faith? You only know that *you have faith when you remove the stone—when you do the thing that God has asked you to do.* If you're not doing the thing that He told you to do, then you're not having faith. If you're discussing it, you're not at the point of faith yet; you're at the point of discussion. If you're thinking about it, you're not at the point of faith yet; you're at the point of thought.

You are not at the point of faith until God sees that stone move.

What can you expect to happen when you move the stone? Jesus told Martha that if she will believe, she will see the "glory of God." The glory of God is seeing God manifest Himself in your situation. You will see God show up in your rock-and-a-hard-place scenario.

DON'T SEEK THE DETAILS

But it's important, also, to note what Jesus did not say Martha would see. While Jesus does tell Martha that something is going to happen, He does not give her the details of what that something will be.

That's important to realize. Many of us go to God and say, "God, tell me what You are going to do behind the stone when I move it so that I can decide if it's worth me moving the stone. Give me the details, and then I'll exercise my faith." But what we need to remember is another deep, but simple, theological principle: If God doesn't get us to respond to His revealed will—"remove the stone"—we will never get to see His secret will. You will never know what He's going to do behind the stone until you move the stone. As long as you keep discussing the stone, it will always be a secret. God says, "Remove the stone, then I'll show you what I'm going to do in secret behind the stone."

A lot of us are not seeing what God can do because we not only want God to tell us what He is going to do first, we also want to discuss moving the stone with everyone around us. We want to discuss the possible outcomes of our obedience instead of getting around to doing the obedience. We want to discuss the potential downfalls of God's request just like Martha. Martha had told Jesus, "Hey, if we remove the stone, it's going to stink."

Martha's statement can apply to many of us because many of us are in a stinky situation. It's smelly. So what do we do? We come up with meetings to discuss moving the stone. We meet too much. A lot of these meetings only need to be one meeting; all we're going to discuss in the second or third meeting is the same stone. We'll discuss that maybe we should put the stone on one end and scoot it out just a bit first. Or we'll discuss how many people will be needed to move the stone. We'll discuss how some of us just don't feel like moving the stone in the morning. Some of us would prefer to move it at night. Ten years later and we're still discussing moving the same stone a thousand different ways. While we're having our meetings year after year, guess what's happening behind the stone? Stuff is getting stinkier.

JESUS, OUR GREAT GO–BETWEEN

John 11:41 tells us the funeral party finally got it. "So they removed the stone." Without any more discussion, they removed the stone. The next word in the passage is critical. It says, "Then . . . " After they did what Jesus told them to do, Jesus did His thing. Jesus did not do His thing until after they had removed the stone.

We read, "Then Jesus raised His eyes, and said, 'Father, I thank You that You have heard Me. I knew that You always hear Me; but because of the people standing around I said it, so that they may believe that You sent Me'" (vv. 41–42).

A great truth in the Bible from the book of Hebrews shows up in the verse we just read. Hebrews 7 speaks of Jesus when it says, "Therefore He is able also to save forever those who draw near to God through Him, since He always lives to make intercession for them" (v. 25). To intercede for somebody is to be a go-between. A lawyer in a courtroom is an intercessor for the client. Jesus is our go-between.

Recall from chapter 7 Martha's words: "'Even now I know that whatever You ask of God, God will give You'" (John 11:22). Martha took what she had learned and knew that the Father would do whatever Jesus asked. Obviously she was not getting through; so she asked Jesus to step in and talk to the Father for her to bring about a change in her situation.

The Bible declares that Jesus is seated on the right hand of the Father, where He "also intercedes for us" (Romans 8:34). That is a theological concept that seems ethereal to most of us. But if you can grasp that truth and apply it to your relationship with God, it can change everything. Because if you will remove the stone, simply do the thing Jesus has revealed to you to do—and you can discover what that is by abiding in Christ—then Jesus will talk to God for you.

Let me tell you the difference between when you talk to God and when Jesus talks to God for you. When you talk to God, you may or may not get through based on the purity of your life or a lot of different circumstances. But when Jesus talks to God for you, God always hears Him. Jesus stood before Lazarus' tomb and said to His Father, "I knew that You always hear Me" (v. 42). The key to prayer is Jesus praying on behalf of what you are asking for. That's why He says, "If you abide in Me, and My words abide in you, ask whatever you wish, and it will be done for you" (John 15:7). Jesus is giving you the privilege of piggybacking on His faith. Like the illustration of the little girl climbing onto her daddy's back (in chapter 1), Jesus is saying, "Even if your faith is weak, piggyback on Me."

How do you do that?

Abide in Him. Discover what God's viewpoint is on the matter. Learn what He is asking you to do through His Word. Then do it; remove the stone. Remove it, as the funeral party did when Jesus asked them to. Jesus prayed. God responded.

We read, "When He had said these things, He cried out with a loud voice, 'Lazarus, come forth'" (v. 43). Now, I'm sure glad Jesus said, "*Lazarus*, come forth" because if He would have just said, "Come forth" then all of the dead in their graves would have gotten up and out of there.

But Jesus called one name. Jesus made it personal. Jesus called forth a specific person in a specific situation in response to specific faith exercised by specific people. Guess what those specific people got? They got a resurrection. They got a miracle.

Lazarus was trapped in a grave, and only God could get him out.

REMOVE THE STONE

I wonder if you have ever been trapped in a grave? Has your rock-and-a-hard-place situation brought about a death somehow? You've tried to walk out of the tomb on your own, but it just keeps dragging you back. You are trapped. Stuck. If this describes your situation, you need more than resuscitation. You need more than deliverance. You need a resurrection. Do you remember what Jesus said to a dead situation? He said, "Come forth."

God wants to make some dead scenarios come forth. He wants to make dead careers come alive once more. He wants to resurrect dead marriages. He just can't get husbands and wives to remove the stone. They want to keep talking about all of this other stuff when God says, "All you need to do is remove the stone."

Martha and Mary didn't make life come forth. All they did was remove the stone at His word. Then He created a miracle.

Someone reading this book needs a miracle. Something in your life has died, and you need God to call it back to life. Someone is trapped in an addiction. You've tried everything that you know to get out of it but it doesn't seem to work. What you need is a resurrection. Someone is trapped in a poor self-image. You've tried what the counselors and self-help books and television programs have told you to do but you are still trapped. What you need is a resurrection.

God can take your dead or dying scenario and call forth a resurrection. He can take what looks like a rotting situation and give it new life. He's just waiting for you to remove the stone. When we do what God says to do in faith, God is free to bring forth life.

CALL ON THE RIGHT NOW GOD

That's great news that can give you courage when you're caught between a rock and a hard place. Remember what Abraham, Moses, the Israelites, the disciples, and Mary and Martha learned—that the God you trust in, sing to, read and hear about is the I Am God. He is the Right Now God for your trick-bag trial. As dead as it may look doesn't mean that's as dead as it has to be. As hopeless as it may appear doesn't mean that's as hopeless as it really is. It just may mean that God is waiting for you to remove the stone. Ask Him if you don't know what stone He wants you to remove. Tell Him you are willing to do it if He will reveal to you through His Word what He wants you to do.

Martha had the mourners remove the stone.

Jesus called Lazarus by name.

Lazarus, who once was dead, got up again.

God wants to be the same all-powerful, I Am God for you. God wants to give you more than theology. He wants to give you an experience with Himself. He wants to be real to you. Having a medical book is nice. Having a doctor is better. Having a menu is nice. Having a meal is better.

When you go to a restaurant, someone brings you a written description of what they have to offer. It's written down and you can read it for yourself. Sometimes you salivate just reading the menu because it looks so good. But you're not satisfied enough to leave the restaurant just having read the menu because you didn't go to the restaurant just to read.

Next, a waiter will come over to you and proclaim the menu to you. The waiter will walk down all aspects of the menu and exegete it for you. The waiter will tell you what different terms mean, how stuff is made, and even give you his personal view of what he likes to eat. But you are still not satisfied because you didn't go to the restaurant to hear somebody else preach about it. You will be satisfied only when you have tasted what the restaurant has to offer you.

LET CHRIST CALL FORTH
THE DEAD AND DYING

In John 11 Jesus says that He wants to give you a taste for yourself that He is the Right Now, I Am God. Reading about Him is good. Hearing about Him is good. But if you leave this life without having deeply experienced the God of your rock-and-a-hard-place situation, then you will never have known all that He can do for you. You will have missed the "something significant" that He has planned for you. You will never know what it is like to hear the God who created the Universe call your trick-bag scenario by name. You will never know the power in hearing Him say, "Marriage, come forth. Health, come forth. Hope, come forth. Family, come forth. Stability, come forth. Joy, come forth. Peace, come forth. Career, come forth. Finances, come forth."

Whatever is dead or dying in your life can be called forth. Jesus can call even dead things back to life. And the excellent part about that is when Christ does, you won't need somebody else to tell you how great God can be because you will have seen Him for yourself.

God longs to be more than just theology on a shelf. He wants to be real to you right now. To accomplish this, sometimes He allows us to get, or even puts us, between a rock and a hard place. He lets something die for the express purpose of letting us experience a resurrection. Because God knows that when we see Him for who He really is, we will never see life the same again.

God wants us to view all of life differently, even the ordinary experiences that we face. He wants us to view them through spiritual eyes rather than through the eyes of a physical world that defines our existence day by day. The reason why we're not experiencing more resurrections is because we are too earthbound, so tied to the physical definitions and expectations of life that we miss the spiritual. Because we are too earthbound, we don't remove the stone.

But today, if you are sick of your cemetery or claustrophobic in your casket, all it takes is for you to remove the stone. Find out from God's Word what He wants you to do. Tell Him that you will do it even though you don't like it, don't understand it, or it doesn't make sense. Do it anyway in faith. Then watch your faith be made sight.

It's time for a resurrection. Are you going to remove the stone?

IN THE HARD PLACES

1. Jesus' tears, recorded in John 11:35, are just one sign of His empathy with men and women. In what other ways did Jesus show his feelings and limits while on earth, according to the section "Jesus Feels Our Pain"?

2. What parts of God's strategy for taking the walled city of Jericho seemed illogical? What was the point, then, of Joshua and his men following God's instructions?

3. According to the section "Live by Faith," how do you know you have faith?

4. In chapter 1 we saw a little girl's faith by riding piggyback on her dad. In this final chapter we are told to have faith to ride piggyback on the shoulders of Jesus. How do you do that?

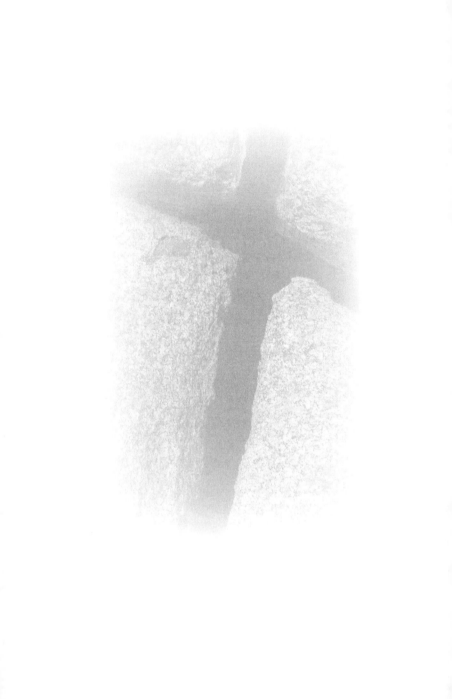

ACKNOWLEDGMENTS

THANKS TO MY GOOD FRIEND Greg Thornton, vice president of Moody Publishers, and to the entire Moody Publishers team for the many years of ministry we have shared together.

MARRIAGE MATTERS

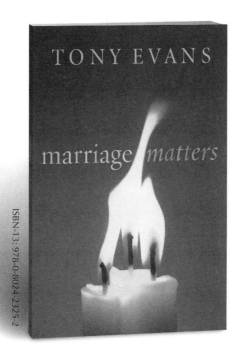

Marriage Matters examines the nature of the covenant, or agreement, we enter into on our wedding day. This booklet provides the foundation for the booklets *For Married Women Only* and *For Married Men Only*, as Evans looks to the Scriptures to define what a covenant is, who makes it, and what the implications are. Let the practical and engaging Tony Evans lead you in knowing just how much...Marriage Matters.

MOODY
PUBLISHERS
moodypublishers.com

FOR MARRIED MEN ONLY

FOR MARRIED WOMEN ONLY

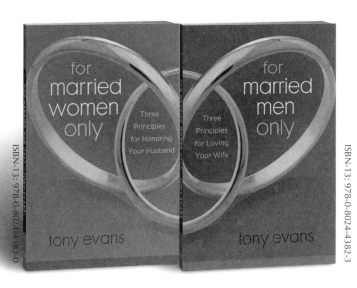

ISBN-13: 978-0-8024-4383-0

ISBN-13: 978-0-8024-4382-3

How is a wife to love her husband? By learning three things, says Tony Evans: how to submit, seduce, and surrender to her husband. Out of these three principles a godly marriage willgrow. Straight-forward yet encouraging.

What does it mean for a husband to love his wife? Three things, says Tony Evans: a husband must be his wife's savior, sanctifier, and satisfier. It is by living out these three principles that a godly marriage will blossom and flourish.

MOODY
PUBLISHERS
moodypublishers.com